Melchizedek

By Donald Peart

Melchizedek©Donald Peart 2020

ISBN: 9798620831180

Scriptural references are:

King James Version, New King James Version, New International Version, New American Standard Bible, Berean Study Bible, English Standard Version

All bold text and literal parenthetical phrases in the Scripture references are added by the author for clarity. Single quotes are also used in some text to highlight a literal definition of the original texts. Some Old English words in the King James Version ("Public Domain") were updated to reflect the modern spelling of those words

Dictionary and Greek reference, includes, but not limited to, Strong's Concordance, Vines Expository Dictionary, BibleWorks Software, ISA2 Basic Software, and BibleHub.com.

Table of Contents

Preface

I though it fit to preface this book with a short write-up. This book is in no wise exhaustive of the Melchizedek order. I have attempted to keep this book as simplistic as possible; because as the writer of the book of Hebrews said, understanding concerning Melchizedek is "difficult to interpret" (or lit., "difficult to 'translate'"). Yet, the Melchizedek priesthood is foremost understood by the "translation" of Hebrew words, and "interpreting" the hieroglyphics of ancient Hebrew letters and words, as we will see later in this book. That is, "skill in the word of righteousness" is needed to fully understand the Melchizedek order.

However, for those who may not be "skillful in the Word of righteousness," citing too many Scriptures make it more difficult to understand. Therefore, I have purposely limited Scripture references, to foster easy reading. So, as you read this book, it may be simple to some, yet it may be meat to those who are being introduced to "this Melchizedek" order. That is, it may difficult to follow some of the interpreting concepts concerning "this Melchizedek."

The writer of the book of Hebrews made it clear that the teaching about Melchizedek is considered as "meat," and not "milk." In fact, the "meat" teaching of "this Melchizedek" is for those who have been "probed-tested" in the Word of righteousness.

So again, I have kept this book simple, and repeated some concepts with a view to develop understanding.

Hebrews 7:1-2,NASB: **¹For this** *Melchizedek, king of Salem, priest of the Most High God, ... was first of all, by the* **translation of his name**, *king of righteousness, and then also king of Salem, which is king of peace.*

*Hebrews 5:6-14, ESV: [6]as he says also in another place, "You are a priest forever, after the order of **Melchizedek.**" [7]In the days of his flesh, Jesus offered up prayers and supplications, with loud cries and tears, to him who was able to save him from death, and he was heard because of his reverence. [8]Although he was a son, he learned obedience through what he suffered. [9]And being made perfect, he became the source of eternal salvation to all who obey him, [10]being designated by God a high priest after the order of Melchizedek. [11]About this we have much to say, and it is **hard to explain,** since you have become dull of hearing. [12]For though by this time you ought to be teachers, you need someone to teach you again the basic principles of the oracles of God. **You need milk, not solid food,** [13]for everyone who lives on milk is **unskilled** in **the word of righteousness,** since he is a child. [14]But solid food is for the mature, for those who have their powers of discernment trained by constant practice to distinguish good from evil.*

Jesus, Our Melchizedek

The name Melchizedek is used eleven (11) times in the Bible. It is used two (2) times in the Old Testament, and nine (9) in the New Testament. Melchizedek was a type of Jesus Christ, the Son of the living God, who is also our High Priest. Hebrews 5:6, declares that **Jesus** is **"a priest forever after the order of Melchizedek."** Hebrews 6:20 also declares "Jesus was made a **High Priest** forever after the order of Melchizedek." In Hebrews 7:3, we see that Melchizedek was also "made like unto the Son of God"— Jesus.

> *14 For it is evident that **our Lord** sprang out of **Judah;** of which tribe Moses spoke nothing concerning priesthood. 15 And it is yet far more evident: for that **after the similitude of Melchizedek** there arises another priest, 16 Who is made, not after the law of a carnal commandment, but after the power of an endless life. 17 For he testifies, **You** are a priest forever after the order of **Melchizedek** (Hebrews 7:14-17).*

> *5 So also **Christ** glorified not himself to be made a **High Priest;** but He that said to him, You are **my Son,** today have I begotten You. 6 As he says also in another place, **You are a priest forever after the order of Melchizedek** (Hebrews 5:5-6).*

The references above is clear! The Father of Heaven appointed His Son, Jesus Christ, our High Priest, over a His own priesthood (us). Jesus' High Priesthood and His priests under Him, the Church of the living God, is according to the order of Melchizedek. Thus, the Church of Jesus Christ must understand the mystery of the Melchizedek order, as he relates to the ministry of Jesus and Jesus' Church.

Who is this Melchizedek who is **"made like"** (or lit., 'from-same') as Jesus? What is the order of Melchizedek, relative to Jesus? What is the function of the Melchizedek's priesthood concerning Jesus? What is the three-fold manifestation of Melchizedek, as he relates to Jesus? Where is Melchizedek, who typifies Jesus, our Forerunner? What is the Melchizedek principle relative to tithing? How does the Melchizedek relate to the millennium rule of Christ and His resurrected priests ruling with Christ? What is the definition of "priest?"

Melchizedek, First Mention

Genesis 14:17-20: ^{17}*And the king of Sodom went out to meet [Abram] after his return from the slaughter of Chedorlaomer, and of the kings that were with him, at the valley of Shaveh, which is the king's dale.* ^{18}*And **Melchizedek king of Salem brought forth bread and wine: and he was the priest of the 'Highest' God.** ^{19}And he blessed him, and said, blessed be Abram of the 'Highest' God, possessor of heaven and earth:* ^{20}*And blessed be the Highest God, which has delivered your enemies into your hand. And he gave him tithes of all.*

In the reference above we see the "first mention" of Melchizedek. Prior to this first mention, nothing is said of him before he was revealed to Abram in Genesis 14. **However, the mystery that surrounds Melchizedek, in this first mention of him, can now be understood because of the crucifixion of Jesus.** We have learned that the first mention of Melchizedek in the New Testament, Hebrews 5:5-7, is about Jesus and Jesus' emotional suffering. In the process of providing insight about Melchizedek, as a type of Jesus Christ, the author of the book of Hebrews used the **"translation"** of Melchizedek's name, and the City Melchizedek ruled as the introduction to the understanding of the Melchizedek's priesthood.

Hebrews 7:1-2, NASB: ^{1}*For this Melchizedek, king of Salem, priest of the Most High God, who met Abraham as he was returning from the slaughter of the kings and blessed him,* ^{2}*to whom also Abraham apportioned a tenth part of all the spoils, was first of all, by the **translation of his name**, king of righteousness, and then also king of Salem, which is king of peace.*

So, the translation of the Hebrew words relating to Melchizedek is an integral part of understanding the mystery of Melchizedek. With that said, in Genesis 14:18-20 these layers of truth are introduced about Melchizedek.

1. Melchizedek is the king of Salem
2. Melchizedek bought forth bread and wine
3. Melchizedek is a priest of the Highest God
4. Melchizedek blessed Abram
5. Melchizedek blessed the Highest God the Possessor of heaven and earth
6. Melchizedek blessed the Highest God for delivering Abram's enemies into Abram hands
7. Melchizedek received Abram's tithe

Now let us look at the interpretation and/or translation of each item above, plus one, in a basic way.

1. Melchizedek bought forth "bread and wine." According to Jesus, communion bread and communion wine represents the body of Jesus which was broken for us, and the blood of Jesus which was poured out for us. Therefore, Melchizedek bought forth the communion principle Jesus to Abram.
2. King of Salem is translated as King of Peace that relates to the "peace 'of' God" and "peace 'with' God," through Jesus, "our peace"
3. In addition to being king, Melchizedek was a "priest of the Highest God." This mean he represented Jesus' King-Priest ministry; Jesus being "set at [Gods'] right hand in the heavenly **far above all.**" Priests "reveal the yes" to God's people; or priest reveal the "it-is-so." Priest minister in things pertaining to God.
4. Melchizedek "blessed" Abram, who includes blessings upon all the "seed" who was in "Abraham," both the natural seed, Israel, and the spiritual seed, Jesus' Church.
5. Melchizedek blessed the Highest God and recognized God' absolute ownership of heaven and earth.
6. He blessed the Highest God, for delivering Abram enemies into Abram's hand. Thus, the Melchizedek order also deals with war and warriors.

7. Melchizedek received Abram's tithe. The Church is to tithe to the Melchizedek's priesthood.
8. "Melchizedek" is a Hebrew compound word made up of "melek" (king) and zadok (righteousness). Hence, as indicated in Hebrew 7:2, he typifies Jesus, who is the King of Righteousness.

The Oath (God's Seven)

*Psalms 110:4: The LORD has **sworn (lit., seven),** and will not repent, You are a priest forever after the **order** of Melchizedek.*

Concerning Jesus, the Christ, the Son of the living God, the heavenly Father took an **"oath"** stating that the Lord Jesus Christ is "a Priest forever after the **order of Melchizedek."** The Hebrew definition for **"oath"** means **to seven oneself.** Thus, the order of Melchizedek is quoted **seven** time in the Bible, to coincide with God's oath concerning Jesus and His royal priesthood. Let us, review the oath (seven) of God towards Jesus Christ.

First Oath!

*Psalms 110:4: The LORD has **sworn (lit., seven),** and will not repent, You are a priest forever after the **order of Melchizedek.***

The oath (lit. to seven oneself) of Melchizedek, in Psalm 110:4, was the first-mention of the "order of Melchizedek." Jesus also specifically referenced Psalm 110, in Matthew 22:41-46. In His reference, Jesus linked Psalm 110 to Jesus being "Lord" to king David, and at the same time being David's "son." Jesus also used Psalm 110 in reference to His enemies being made His footstool.

Why did I cite Jesus' reference of His life to king David?" King David was not only a man of worship, but king David was also a man of war. In fact, Psalm 110 that first reference of the order of Melchizedek is a depiction of Jesus seated at the right hand of the Father, until all of Jesus enemies is made His footstool through war.

Saying another way, the order of Melchizedek, is also an order of war against heavenly principalities, heavenly authorities, world-governments of the darkness of this age, and spiritual hurts upon the heavens. Paul said these are the enemies we wrestle against. The last enemy to be destroyed is death. It is also written that "the **weapons** of our **warfare** are not fleshly, but mighty through God." With that said, remember that Melchizedek met Abram just after Abraham waged war, and the Lord had "delivered Abram's enemies into his hands." So, the Melchizedek order will also have to confront fleshly enemies, as will be discussed later in this book.

Second Oath!

*Hebrew 5:6: As He says also in another, You a priest forever after the **order of** Melchizedek.*

Hebrew 5:6 is the second-mention of the order of Melchizedek in the Bible, but the first-mention in the New Testament. The context of this "oath" (all of Hebrews, chapter 5) is that of the "calling" of Jesus as God's High Priest. This call relates to the following:

1. Jesus offering Himself as a sacrifice for our sins.
2. Jesus' ability to "measure our emotional sufferings;" and thus, bringing emotional and physical healing and release to the spirit, soul, and bodies of humanity.

Thus, the calling of Jesus as Melchizedek is with an "oath" that cannot be broken, Jesus is or High Priest in things pertaining to God on our behalf, forever!

Third Oath!

*Hebrew 5:9-10: ^{9}And being made perfect, he became the author of **eternal salvation** unto all them that obey him; ^{10}**Called of** God a High Priest after the **order of** Melchizedek.*

The reference of this "oath" first references Jesus being called to "marketplace." **"Called"** is a Greek compound word (prosagoreuo, "towards (pros)" and "marketplace (agora)." An "agora" was also an assembling place related to athletics, military musters, legislations, and politics. Yes, Jesus' High priesthood also functions in the marketplace. It follows that Jesus' royal priesthood (His Church) also have a ministry in the marketplace. And for those who do not agree with marketplace ministry, or understand the priestly ministry relative to the marketplace, be mindful not to persecute those of Christ who have a legitimate ministry in the marketplace. Would you agree that Joseph Moses, Joshua, Deborah, David, Barak, Daniel, and so on had a ministry related to the marketplace?

Secondly, this third use of the oath (to seven oneself) is in reference to Jesus becoming the "Causer" and the "Author" of **eternal salvation**. There are basically three stages of "things that accompany salvation," the "common salvation," (applies to all who believes that **Jesus is the Christ);** the "great salvation" (the salvation that manifest Jesus' miraculous signs and wonders); and the "eternal salvation" (the salvation that covers resurrection life, translation, deathlessness, eternal life). Jesus is the "Causer" of all the things that accompany salvation.

Fourth Oath!

*Hebrew 6:20: 'Where' the **forerunner** is for us entered, even Jesus, made a High Priest forever after the **order of Melchizedek.***

The oath of Melchizedek also prefigures Jesus as our **forerunner** into the Holy of Holies. "Forerunner" can be defined as a person who precedes the development (maturity) of someone else. That is, as Melchizedek was "carried-through" into heaven, so likewise, Jesus has entered into the heavens in the presence of God as one who has ran ahead of us, and He expects us to mature as Him, and follow Him into **"that** within the veil." As we will see later in this text, **"that** within the veil" that Jesus foreran for us relates to the Church fulfilling the function of priests, as Jesus also went ahead of us functioning as our "Great Priest." Part of the priestly function relates to Jesus' defeat of Satan, and

Jesus "High Priest" ministry relating to the compassionate atonement the Lord secured for us.

Fifth Oath!

*Hebrews 7:11: If therefore **'maturity'** were by the Levitical priesthood, (for under it the people **received the law**,) what further need that another priest should rise after the **order of Melchizedek**, and not be called after the order of Aaron?*

Jesus is now the Lawgiver that leads us to maturity, according to the order of Melchizedek. That is, the fifth reference of the order of Melchizedek, is linked to "maturity," "legislating," and "tithing."

Without getting into different layers of truth, the order of Melchizedek establishes legislation that fosters maturity. For example, Jesus, in Matthew 5, legislated and refined Moses' law with a view to walking maturely. Jesus said, "**43You have heard that it has been said,** you shall love your neighbor, and hate your enemy. **44But I say** to you, love your enemies, bless them that curse you, do good to them that hate you, and pray for them which despitefully use you, and persecute you" (Matthew 5:43-44).

Moses gave the law that Jesus referenced above, however, Jesus legislated further, showing a more mature expression of love. This is a function of the Melchizedek order; it brings clarity to God's laws that causes spiritual growth. In addition, the fifth oath also relates to tithing.

*Hebrews 7:4-11: 4Now consider how great this man was, unto whom even the patriarch **Abraham gave the tenth** of the spoils. 5And verily they that are of the sons of Levi, who receive the office of the priesthood, **have a commandment to take tithes** of the people according to the law, that is, of their brethren, though they come out of the loins of Abraham: 6But he whose* *descent is not counted from them received tithes of Abraham, and blessed him that had the promises. ⁷And without all contradiction the less is blessed of the better. ⁸And here men that die receive tithes; but there he receives them, of whom it is witnessed that he lives. ⁹And as I may so say, Levi also, who receives tithes, payed tithes in Abraham. ¹⁰For he was yet in the loins of his father when* **Melchizedek** *met him. ¹¹If therefore* **'maturity'** *was by the Levitical priesthood, (for under it the people received the law,) what further need was there that another priest should rise after* **the order of Melchizedek,** *and not be called after the order of Aaron?*

In the Old Testament, the people tithe to the priests, Aaron, and his sons. In the New Testament, Jesus is our High Priest, and we are to tithe to Jesus' ministry and to His brothers. Jesus did **not** eliminate tithe, in fact, He said it is not to be left undone (Matthew 23:23). Also, we walk in maturity when we tithe. It is a part of the law of maturity to tithe! With that said, there are two items that need to be understood concerning tithing (again, I will keep this as simple as possible).

1. When we tithe to the ministry of Jesus, we are testifying that Jesus is indeed alive.
    > *And here men that die receive* **tithes;** *but there he receives them, of whom it is* **witnessed that he lives** *(Hebrews 7:8).*

Melchizedek is still alive, who received tithe from Abraham some four thousand (4,000) years ago. The same is true of Jesus our Melchizedek; as we tithe, we testify that Jesus is alive. Yes, we serve, the living God! There is a real live flesh and bone Jesus in the heavens, and in us; and we testify to the world that he lives when we tithe to Jesus' Church. Conversely, when a person does not tithe, that person may be implying that Jesus is not alive to him/her.

2. Tithing bless your offspring, even while they are in your loins.

> *⁹And as I may so say, Levi also, who receives tithes, payed tithes in Abraham. ¹⁰For he was **yet in the loins of his father when** Melchizedek met him (Hebrews 7:9-10).*

One of the reasons the Levites receives tithe, in addition to God choosing them, is that the blessing of Abraham was passed to them, because they were in Abraham's loins when Abraham tithed to Melchizedek. This principle of transference of blessing is not isolated. When the angel spoke with Jacob in Genesis 32, a prophet said that God spoke to all Israel, while they were un-fathered.

> *³He [Jacob] took his brother [Esau] by the heel in the womb, and by his strength he had power with God: ⁴Yea, he had power over the angel, and prevailed: he wept, and made supplication unto him: he found him in Bethel, **and there he spoke with us** (Hosea 12:3-4).*

Yes, like Abraham, Jacob's blessings were passed to his offspring, even though the offspring was not birthed at the time of the promise. This is also true with respect to Jesus. All of Jesus' seed is blessed through Jesus.

> *That the blessing of Abraham might come on the Gentiles through Jesus Christ; that we might receive the promise of the Spirit through faith (Galatians 3:14).*

Through Jesus, no believer is cursed, regardless of ethnicity. All races are blessed through Jesus, the Son of the living God

The fifth oath of God also relates to "maturity" that comes through the Melchizedek order. This maturity, as mentioned in the book of Hebrews, relates to mature conscience, maturity of eternal resurrection from the dead, maturity of re-legislating the

13

qualification to be High Priest and the "priest-togetherness." With that said, lets us briefly discuss the mature conscience that can only be realized through the blood of Jesus and the eternal Spirit.

> How much more shall **the blood of Christ**, who through the eternal Spirit offered himself without spot to God, **purge your conscience** from dead works to serve the living God? (Hebrews 9:14)

The blood of Jesus "purges the conscience from dead works," and the "consciousness of evil," freeing us to serve God without condemnation. One of the marks of maturity is a person who is not self-rejected by carrying undue burdens of being sin-conscious, demon-conscious, self-conscious; evil-conscious, **but rather they demonstrate maturity by being God conscious!** That is, they understand that Jesus has permanently cleanse them of their sins and their past transgression; "and therefore, have no more conscience of sins" (contrast Hebrews 10:1-2 with 10:22).

Sixth Oath!

*Hebrew 7:17: For He testifies, You a priest **forever** after the **order of Melchizedek**.*

The sixth manifestation of God's oath relates to Jesus being the High "priest forever." The Greek text reads as such: "You are a priest '**into the age**' 'according-to' the order of Melchizedek." Thus, "forever" is the same as living "into the age." Jesus used this phase ("into the age") regularly in His teaching when speaking of the resurrection "age to come." Here is an example:

*John 6:50-51: ⁵⁰This is the bread which comes down from heaven, that a man may eat thereof, and **not die**. ⁵¹I am the living bread which came down from heaven: if any man eats of this bread, he shall live **forever (lit., into the age)**: and the bread*

14

that I will give is my flesh, which I will give for the life of the world.

There are many ages; in addition, there also exist "that age," or "the age." This "age" is both a literal age and a spiritual state or spiritual place. With that said, we are currently at the close of the sixth (6th) one-thousand-year age, starting from the first Adam. We are about to enter another age (the age to come). This age to come is also the Sabbath Age, or the millennium referenced in Revelation 20. In addition, this "age" is also a literal "place" in the Spirit, in the heavens. That is, "into the age" relative to Melchizedek is the place of the heavenly Holy of Holies, and all the atonement, authority, power, love, mercy, kindness that comes with being currently seated-together with Jesus in that "age;" with the understanding that when this current age is completed and the age to come arrives, we will also live in that age literally.

Ephesians 2:6-7, BSB: ⁶And God raised us up with Christ and **seated us with Him** *in the heavenly realms in Christ Jesus, ⁷in order that in the* **coming ages** *He might display the surpassing riches of His grace, demonstrated by His kindness to us in Christ Jesus.*

Hebrews 6:17-20: ¹⁷Wherein God, willing more abundantly to show to the heirs of promise the immutability of his counsel, confirmed it by an oath: ¹⁸That by two immutable things, in which it was impossible for God to lie, we might have a strong consolation, who have fled for refuge to lay hold upon the hope set before us: ¹⁹Which we have as an anchor of the soul, both sure and steadfast, and which enters into that **within the veil;** *²⁰Where the forerunner is for us entered,* **Jesus,** *made an* **high priest 'into the age'** *after the* **order of Melchizedek.**

Hebrews 10:19-22, BSB: ¹⁹Therefore, brothers, since we have confidence to enter **the Most Holy Place** *by the blood of Jesus, ²⁰by the new and living way opened for us through the curtain of*

*His body, [21]and since we have a **great priest** over the house of God, [22]let us draw near with a sincere heart in full assurance of faith, having our hearts sprinkled to cleanse us **from a guilty conscience** and our bodies washed with pure water.*

Briefly summing up the references above, Jesus forerunning "within the veil" is the same as Jesus filling (entering) His people with His Spirit. It is the same as Jesus entering "into the age;" and it is the same as Jesus entering the heavenly Holies of Holies.

Seventh Oath!

*Hebrew 7:21: (For those priests were made without an oath; but this with an oath by Him that said to Him, the Lord swore and **will not repent,** You a priest forever after the **order of Melchizedek:***

The phrase "will not repent," also mean, "will not regret." God, the heavenly Father, has "no regrets" with regards to His Son Jesus, the Christ, being the High Priest forever (into the age) according to the order of Melchizedek. However, in Genesis we read that God "regretted" that he made mankind who corrupted themselves and corrupted the earth; a corruption that is linked to the illegal offspring of the sons of God, and mankind's imagination being "evil all day."

However, God has no regrets concerning the High Priest ministry of Jesus! Jesus did not disappoint His heavenly Father! Jesus, the Son of the living God, fulfilled the Father's will as Priest unto God; and Jesus is still fulfilling His High priestly function. The same is true for us, the heavenly Father has no regret towards you, if we remain in Jesus. We are accepted (or highly favored) in the Beloved Son, Jesus.

Ephesians 1:3-7: [3]Blessed be the God and Father of our Lord Jesus Christ, who has blessed us with all spiritual blessings in heavenly places in Christ: [4]**According as** he hath chosen us in him before the foundation of the world, that we should be holy and without blame before him in love: [5]Having predestinated us unto **'son-placing'** by Jesus Christ to himself, according to the good pleasure of his will, [6]To the praise of the glory of his grace, wherein he has **made us accepted (or highly favored)**[1] **in the beloved.** [7]In whom we have redemption through his blood, the forgiveness of sins, according to the riches of his grace.

---

[11] "Charitoo," used only twice in the Bible Luke 1:28 and Ephesians 1:6

The Order of Melchizedek

As we previously learned, Melchizedek was introduced to the Church by the writer of the book of Hebrews by "translating" Melchizedek's name, and "translating" the name of the City he ruled. Thus, the "translation" of words relating to Melchizedek is a principle that is to be maintained as we seek to understand the mystery of Melchizedek.

Thus, I will be showing from the Hebrew pictographic language, layers of truth concerning Melchizedek. Not only was he a type of Jesus, but he also preached Jesus to Abram; and declared the "word" of Jesus to Abram. The order of Melchizedek is the preaching of Jesus Christ, the Son of the living God, who was crucified for us. The order of Melchizedek serves bread and wine, which is the communion of the body and the blood of Jesus for His believers.

The Body and Blood of Jesus

Genesis 14:18-19: *¹⁸And Melchizedek king of Salem **brought forth bread and wine: and he was the priest of the 'Highest' God.** ¹⁹And he blessed him, and said, blessed be Abram of the 'Highest' God, possessor of heaven and earth:*

Matthew 26:26-28: *²⁶And as they were eating, Jesus took **bread**, and blessed it, and broke it, and gave it to the disciples, and said, **take, eat; this is my body.** ²⁷And he took **the cup,** and gave thanks, and gave it to them, **saying, drink** you all of it; ²⁸For **this is my blood** of the new testament, which is shed for many for the remission of sins.*

God trusted Melchizedek with the mystery of Jesus Christ. Melchizedek was the first to give the communion bread and wine. Abraham was the first to take the communion of Jesus. Jesus declared that "bread" is His "body." Jesus declared that "the cup" of wine is His "blood." Thus, Melchizedek revealed the communion principle to Abram! That is, Melchizedek, preached Jesus and Jesus' crucifixion. He brough forth to Abram the flesh and blood of Jesus that gives life; and this life is linked to the life-making Spirit of the living God (John 6:63).

*John 6:35: And **Jesus said** to them, **I am the bread of life:** he that comes to me shall never hunger; and he that believes 'into' me shall never thirst.*

*John 5:51: **I am the living bread** which came down from heaven: if any man eats of **this bread,** he shall live forever: and the **bread that I will give is my flesh,** which I will give for the life of the world.*

*John 6:53-54: [53] Then Jesus said unto them, 'amen, amen,' I say to you, except you eat the flesh of the Son of man, and **drink his blood,** you have no life in you.[54] Whoso **eats my flesh, and drinks my blood, has eternal life;** and I will raise him up at the last day.*

Through Jesus' truth stated above, and His historical crucifixion, Jesus body and blood were offered for us. Jesus also declared that we could eat his flesh (bread) and drink his blood (wine). So, the question must be asked, how do we eat His flesh and drink His blood? Our Lord said that "coming to Him" is a form of eating, and "believing into Him" is the same as drinking. Thus, Melchizedek bough forth the flesh and blood of Jesus to Abram; and Abram ate the bread and drank the wine.

With that said, there are two ways we can eat the body of Jesus and drink the blood of Jesus.

1. We can eat the bread of Jesus' body and the wine of Jesus' blood by simple taking communion. And yes, if one was to study communion in the Bible, it clearly states that the communion wine is literal wine.
    a. This communion is considered an "expensive dinner," for so the word "supper" is defined. Jesus

paid an expensive price for our redemption, the price of blood!

b. The Scripture declares that if communion is taken unworthy, it may cause "weakness," "sickness," and death ("sleep"). It follows that if communion is taken worthily, it gives us the "strength," "health," and life in the earth (1 Corinthians 11:29-30). Thus, through faith, Abram was given physical strength, health and long life with the communion Melchizedek bought forth to Abram.

2. As I briefly stated above, we can eat the bread of Jesus body by "coming" to Jesus; and we can drink the wine of his blood by "believing into" Jesus.

*John 6:35: And Jesus said to them, I am the bread of life: he that **comes** to me shall **never hunger;** and he that **believes 'into'** me shall never **thirst.***

Jesus made it clear in the text above that "coming" to Jesus is like eating, and therefore, spiritual hunger will be curtailed. Jesus also made it clear that "believing into" Jesus (faith into Jesus) also quenches thirst. Thus, we eat the body of Jesus when we come to Jesus. We drink His blood by simple believing into Him. The promise of doing these things is eternal life, and life "into the age" of the heavenly realm. This is great news! Melchizedek presented to Abram the encouragement to continue to "come" to the Lord and to "believe" into the Lord Jesus! Jesus declared that "Abraham rejoiced to see my (Jesus') day, and he saw it, and was glad!" (John 8:56)

Principles of Interpreting Scriptures

*Psalms 110:4: The LORD has sworn, and will not repent, You are a priest forever after the **order** of Melchizedek.*

We learned previously that writer of the book of Hebrews developed the Melchizedek's doctrine by utilizing the "translation" of Hebrew names into their literal definitions. With this principle of translating the Hebrew language, I will unveil layers of truth concerning the order of Melchizedek as he relates to Jesus. (You may have heard the phrase "truth is like an onion." Each layer has the same ingredient, but it is shaped a little different.) In addition, I would like to remind the reader that Jesus indicated that "the Scriptures ... testify of [Jesus]" (John 5:39). That is, every word and letter of the Scriptures points to Jesus.

"Order" Defined

With that said, what is the "order" of Melchizedek. The order of Melchizedek "testifies of Jesus." The order of Melchizedek is the "Word" of Jesus! The order of Melchizedek is about Jesus the "Door." The order of Melchizedek is about Jesus being crucified! The order of Melchizedek is about the Cross of Christ! The order of Melchizedek preaches Jesus Christ and Him crucified! The order of Melchizedek is the arrangement of Jesus' High Priesthood and His royal priests under Him. Yes, all the above statements, and more, are found in the order of Melchizedek. So, let us look at the **interpretation** of the Hebrew word for "order."

The Hebrew word for **"order"** is (דברתי) DBRTY (reading from right to left). The Hebrew word "order" and its root words are defined in the Strong's Concordance as: **reason, cause, suit, style, word, matter, arrangement, subdue, pestilence.** The Hebrew language is beautiful, and the applications of certain words are vast, as seen in the definition of "order."

1. The Melchizedek priesthood has a "reason" or "cause" in the heavens and in the earth.
2. The Melchizedek priesthood has "style"
3. The Melchizedek priesthood has an "arrangement" (order) they function under.

4. The Melchizedek priesthood executes "pestilence" through the Word of God
5. The Melchizedek priesthood "subdues" their enemies through the Word of God.
6. The Melchizedek ministry preached the Word of God.

Pictograph of "Order" is Jesus

Also, as it is with many languages, Hebrews words are made of letters, and the letters were developed from pictures. The picture for each of the letters in the Hebrew word for "order" (דברתי, DBRTY) used in Psalms 110:4 is as follows:

Deleth (ד)-door, to repeat like a tent door flapping in the wind
Beth (ב)-house, floor plan, household
Resh (ר)-head, mind
Tav (ת)-cross, sign, covenant
Yad (י)-hand (when used at the end of a word it means "my")

Jesus is the **Door**—John 10:7
Jesus is the **House,** and we are His **house**—Hebrews 3:6
Jesus is the **Head**—Colossians 1:18
Jesus is the **crucified** one—2 Corinthians 13:4
Jesus ratified the New **Covenant** in His blood—Matthew 26:28
God's **hand** and counsel predetermined Jesus' crucifixion—Acts 5:28

So, the first layer of truth with respect to the "order" or Melchizedek is this. The Melchizedek order is about the Door (ד), Jesus, His House (ב) (the Church), of which He is the Head (ר), and He was crucified (ת) for His house (including all humanity); and Jesus' crucifixion was predetermined by God's hand (י).

"Order" Word Pictures—Jesus Crucified

The Hebrew word for **"order"** is (דברתי) DBRTY (reading from right to left). Jesus declared that every Scripture, made up of "letters," "testify of Him." Thus, Hebrew letters are pictograph that speaks of Jesus. It follows that the Hebrew word "order" itself points to Jesus Christ, being the **"Son"** of God, the **"Heir"** of God, the **"Wheat"** of God.

That is, the Hebrew word **"order"** (דברתי, DBRTY) has in it the Hebrew word **"BaR"** (בר) which is defined in the King James Version as "son," "heir," and "grain." A good example of "BaR" is Jesus addressing the apostle Peter as "Simon **Bar** Jonah," which means "Simon **heir** of Jonah" or Simon **son** of Jonah," or, Simon **wheat** of Jonah.

With that said, the Hebrew word picture (דברתי) DBRTY may also be read as: **"my-crucified"** (תי), **"Son"** (בר), **"(the) Door."** (ד). Does this sound like Jesus? Yes, the "order" of Melchizedek is about Jesus, God's crucified Son, who is the Door to the heavenly Father. Yes, the "reason" of the Melchizedek "order" is to declare Jesus, as God's crucified Son, the Door.

It follows that when Melchizedek bought forth bread and wine to Abram, Jesus' "order" of priesthood was also demonstrated. That is, Melchizedek's "word" to Abram consisted of Jesus, the Son of the living God; Jesus the crucified-one; and Jesus who also is the Door to the heavenly father; and Jesus and his royal priesthood.

This principle of Melchizedek's order relating to Jesus the Son of God is also witnessed in the New Testament; because the writer of Hebrews declared that Melchizedek was **"made like the Son of God."** The phrase **"made like"** literally reads in the Greek as **"'from-same' the Son of God."** In other words, Melchizedek was fully aware of his sonship, and that he prefigured Jesus, the Son of God.

So, rhetorically, what is the order of Melchizedek? The "order" of Melchizedek is about Jesus, God's crucified Son, the Door. The Melchizedek order is Jesus; and His royal priesthood who preaches the death burial and resurrection of Jesus. The Melchizedek priesthood "preach Christ crucified ... the power of God and the wisdom of God" (1 Corinthians 1:23-24). If one understands this principle of preaching Jesus, then the priesthood of Jesus, must repent from humanistic gospel, and instead preach Jesus crucified and the Church also taking up her cross to follow Jesus!

1 Corinthians 1:23a: But we preach Christ crucified ....

*2 Corinthians 4:5, BSB: For **we do not proclaim ourselves**, but **Jesus Christ as Lord**, and ourselves as your servants for Jesus' sake.*

Genealogy

*Hebrews 7: 1-3, NKJV: ¹For this Melchizedek, king of Salem, priest of the Most High God .... ³**without father, without mother, without genealogy, having neither beginning of days nor end of life,** but made like the Son of God, remains a priest continually.*

Melchizedek was "made like the Son of God." This statement was made with respect to the pedigree of Melchizedek. Melchizedek was "without father, without mother, without genealogy." He did not have "beginning of days, nor end of life." That is, just like Jesus who was birthed through the Holy Spirit and not by physical copulation, Melchizedek was produced out-of God.

From (the) Same

Melchizedek was "made like the Son of God." The phrase literally read Melchizedek was "'from-same' as the Son of God." The Scripture states that Jesus "was come 'out-of' God;" and since Melchizedek was "from (the same) as Jesus; Melchizedek was also generated out-of God. That is, Melchizedek's has the gene of God. Like Jesus, Melchizedek was birthed out of the Spirit of God; and therefore, God is His Father!

Regened

Believers in Jesus Christ have also been regenerated and renewed. That is, all believers in Jesus Christ has been regened. In fact, the Scripture states that regeneration washes us, and the Holy Spirit renews us.

*Titus 1:5b, NKJV: ... according to His mercy **He saved us,** through the **washing of regeneration** and **renewing of the Holy Spirit.***

Regeneration can be defined as regened, re-generated, rebirth, re-genesis, regenerate, and so on. In addition, regeneration, "washes" us. So, the question must be asked, what is washed from us? It appears to me that since God regened us, through washing; then the old genes must have been washed away. "Therefore, if anyone is in Christ, he is a **new creation**; old things have passed away; behold, **all things have become new**" (2 Corinthians 5:17). You are a creation that did not exist before! With this truth established, let us tackle the debate about natural genealogy.

Genealogy Debates

Through the ages, some of mankind has attempted to teach that some ethnic genes are superior to others ethnic genes. All humans are gifted with the gene of God because all humans came from the first Adam, and God created Adam. What most people do not understand is that the thing that affects humans which make is seems like they have so-called inferior gene is not ethnicity.

The Bible is very clear that idolatry, spiritual principalities, and powers in heavenly places have debased all ethnic groups in some way or another. This was a result of Adam hiding from God's love; and thus, he became an **"atheist" (lit., "without-God")**. **Note:** The Bible declares that there exist "the spirit of your mind." Thus, the mind is **also** directly related to "spirit." Thus "spirits" (God's, humans, demonic) can affect the mind, either in advancement or debasement.

God's House-Law

*1 Timothy 1:4, NAS: nor to pay attention to myths and **endless genealogies**, which give rise to mere speculation rather than furthering the **administration (lit., house-law) of** God which is by faith.*

So, with that said, here are the commands of the Bible concerning genealogy. We are not to give heed to "endless genealogy." "Endless," literally means unfinished, un-crossed over, "un-other side;" meaning that any discussion about gene must consider the "other side," which is the "other side" of God's house-law. According to the house-law of regeneration and renewing, God has washed away the effects of sin on humanity's gene; and God's house-law of regening supersedes natural genealogy.

*Titus 1:5b, NKJV: ... according to His mercy **He saved us**, through the **washing of regeneration** and **renewing of the Holy Spirit.***

Avoid Genealogy

*1 Timothy 1:4, NAS: nor to pay attention to myths and **endless genealogies**, which give rise to mere speculation rather than furthering the **administration (lit., house-law)** of God which is by faith.*

*Titus 1:5b, NKJV: ... according to His mercy **He saved us**, through the **washing of regeneration** and **renewing of the Holy Spirit.***

*Titus 3:9, NAS: But **avoid** foolish controversies and **genealogies** and strife and disputes about the Law, **for they are unprofitable and worthless.***

In Titus 3:5, Paul made it clear that we have been regened. And he followed up in Titus 3:9, by saying "avoid genealogies ... for they are unprofitable and vain." Thus, all the talk about people of color having so-called inferior genes is "unprofitable and worthless." Questions about gene only leads to unsuccessful searches! What matters is this! Who is your creator?

Let us settle it:

> *"Whoever believes that Jesus is the Christ is **born of God**, and whoever loves the Father loves the child born of Him (I John 5:1, NAS).*

*^{23}To be renewed in the **spirit of your minds;** ^{24}and to put on the **new self, created** to be **like God** in true righteousness and holiness (Ephesians 4:23-24, BSB).*

You, I, all believers, have God's gene!

Chosen Gene

*1 Peter 2:9a, NAS: But you are **A CHOSEN RACE ....***

"Race" in the reference above is the Greek work "genos," singular for "gene." All who believe into Jesus, is considered a "chosen gene." Thus, the Melchizedek order of priesthood consist of Jesus, the High Priest, **born out-of God's gene;** and the Melchizedek order is a corporate "royal priesthood" under Jesus Christ, **also born out of God's gene.** All believer "were not a people" (they did not have the gene of Jesus); "but now are the people of God" (born-again and regened with Jesus' gene) Yes, all believes have been regened through God's washing. We are a new creation; old things are passed away.

That is, we never existed as we are before God recreated us; and thus, any affected gene has been regenerated through our Melchizedek, Jesus Christ! Your ethnicity does not disqualify you! In fact, your gene qualifies you through Jesus! That is, Jesus' historical gene that includes prostitute, incest, murders, adultery, witchcraft, illegitimate grandparents did not disqualify Him!

*1 Peter 2:9-10, NAS: ^{9}But you are **A CHOSEN RACE (Greek: "genos"),** A royal PRIESTHOOD, A HOLY NATION, A PEOPLE FOR God's OWN POSSESSION, so that you may proclaim the excellencies of Him who has called you out of darkness into His marvelous light; ^{10}for you once were NOT A PEOPLE, but now you are THE PEOPLE OF GOD; you had NOT RECEIVED MERCY, but now you have RECEIVED MERCY.*

Sons of God

Hebrews 7:3, NAS: Without father, without mother, without genealogy, having neither beginning of days nor end of life, but **made like the Son of God,** *he remains a priest perpetually.*

Melchizedek was "made like the Son of God. Again, the Phrase **"made like"** is a Greek compound word that reads **"from-same;"** and it is also defined as "assimilating closely." Thus, Melchizedek not only assimilated Jesus, but he was also from-(the)-same as Jesus.

That is, Melchizedek is "from" God. God is Melchizedek's Father and God is the Father of all the sons of God. Saying it another way, Melchizedek was of the order of sons of God mentioned in Genesis and Job. Like Jesus, Melchizedek was without a natural father, a natural mother, no pedigree; he did not have beginning of days nor end of life.

Priesthood is Sonship

"Sonship" is a synonym for priests. *[5]So also* **Christ** *did not glorify Himself so as to become a* **high priest**, *but He who* **said** *to Him, "YOU ARE MY* **SON**, *TODAY I HAVE BEGOTTEN YOU",[6]just as He says also in another passage, "YOU ARE A* **PRIEST** *FOREVER* **ACCORDING TO THE ORDER OF MELCHIZEDEK** *"(Hebrew 5:5-6, NAS)*

Christ, the High Priest is a function of "the Son." "Son" functions "according to the order of Melchizedek." Melchizedek was "made like the Son of God;" and The Melchizedek High Priest office is the function of "Sonship." Thus, it appears that the sons of God in the Old Testament are related to a priesthood; as the sons of God in the New Testament are also related to Jesus' priesthood. The name of "son" is better than the name angel.

Hebrews 1:4-5: [4]*Being made so much* **better than the angels,** *as he has by inheritance obtained* **a more excellent name than they.** [5]*For unto which of the angels said he at any time,* **You art my Son,** *this day have I 'birthed' you? And again, I will be to him a Father, and he shall be to me a Son?*

Jesus' Sonship is above all angels. The name Son of God is a more excellent name than angels. This is also true for Jesus' spiritual brothers, who are also sons. The believers in this generation have forgotten their identity. Believer's identity as sons, is that of priests to God and mankind. Let us strive to be a son, following the example that Jesus demonstrated to us. Let us walk in the order of Melchizedek, as sons of God declaring the Hight Priesthood of Jesus Christ.

Romans 8:14, NAS: For all who are being led by the Spirit of God, **these are sons of God.**

Galatians 4:6-7, NAS: [6]*Because* **you are sons,** *God has sent forth the Spirit of His Son into our hearts, crying, "Abba! Father!"* [7]*Therefore you are no longer a slave, but a son; and if a son, then an heir through God.*

1 Peter 2:10, NIV, [9]*But you are a chosen people,* **a royal priesthood,** *a holy nation, God's special possession, that you may declare the praises of him who called you out of darkness into his wonderful light.* [10]*Once you were not a people, but now you are the people of God; once you had not received mercy, but now you have received mercy.*

Hebrews 7:17: For he testifies, **You [Jesus]** *are a* **priest** *forever after the order of* **Melchizedek**

Placed Sons of God vs Satan

Job 1:6: Now there was a day when the **sons of God** *came to 'place' themselves before the LORD, and Satan came also 'in-middle-of-them.'*

The Melchizedek priesthood is synonymous with the sons of God. We saw that not only was Melchizedek made like the Son of God, but he was also a son of God, as believers are also considered as sons through Jesus Christ. The sons of God are mentioned in several places in the Old Testament; however, my focus in this section are the sons of God in the book of Job and the book of Genesis

In Job, a familiar phrase is used relative to the sons of God. They came to "place" themselves before the LORD." In the New Testament the phrase "adoption" or "adoption of 'sons'" is used to describe believers; and this phrase **"adoption of sons"** is literally defined as **"sons-placing," or a "placed-sons."**

Thus, in Job 1:6, the "sons of God 'placed' themselves before the Lord" because that was one of their functions as priests. Job 38 also showed that these sons of God were created/birthed before God laid the foundation of the earth (Job 38:5-7). Thus, they were apparently part of the eternal priesthood under Melchizedek.

They were placed sons from old times, and thus, could place themselves before the Lord. In other words, it was their God given "right" as sons of God to place themselves before the Lord. However, Satan apparently also liked to come "in-the-middle-of them;" and according to the Job's record, Satan was there to attack Job.

That is, Satan presence is always to attack sons. Because the definition for Satan" is to "attack." However, according to the apostle Paul, through the God of peace, Satan is crushed under our feet.

Sons of God— "Men-of the-Name"

The sons of God also showed up in Genesis 6; and their presence in Genesis 6 was not in a God context, as they were depicted in

Job 1:6 and Job 38:7. In Genesis 6, some of the sons of God began to choose and try the daughters of men with things related to sex "beyond-fornication," first through dreams. (see Jude). They eventually, married some of Adam's daughters and produced "giants."

*Genesis 6:1-2; 4: ¹And it came to pass, when men began to multiply on the face of the earth, and daughters were born to them, ²That the **sons of God** saw the daughters of men that they were fair; and they took them wives of all which they chose. .... ⁴There were **giants (or, fallen ones)** in the earth in those days; and also, after that, when the sons of God came in unto the daughters of men, and they 'birth' to them, the same mighty men which **'from-eternity,' men of 'the name.'***

In Genesis 6:1-4 context, these sons of God did something forbidden. They married "the daughters of the-Adam," and produced "fallen-ones." In Genesis, 6:4, the original Hebrew text called these sons of God **"mighty-men."** The Hebrew text also gave additional layers of truth. These sons of God were "from-eternity," or literally "from-(the)-concealed." Finally, they were also called "men (or, mortals) of the-name." What name! The name "son."

*Hebrews 1:4-5: ⁴Being made so much better than the angels, as he has by inheritance obtained a **more excellent name** than they. ⁵For unto which of the angels said he at any time, **You are my Son,** this day have I 'birthed' you? And again, I will be to him a Father, and he shall be to me **a Son?***

Yes, these were sons of God, called after "the-name" of the Son. That is, they were eternal priests of the order of sons made like unto the Son of God, according to the order of Melchizedek. Regrettable, some of them corrupted their sonship with sins that was beyond fornication, into acts that caused them to be bound for thousands of years, under darkness, until the Day of Judgment.

Remember, Melchizedek is "made like the Son of God;" and Melchizedek **did not** sin like some of the other sons of God. With the understanding that Jesus, our Melchizedek, did not fall into the sins of men, even though Jesus was "tempted at all points like us!" That is, Melchizedek did not corrupt "the-name," "Son of God."

*Hebrews 4:15-16: [15]For we have not a High Priest which cannot be touched with the feeling of our infirmities; but was in all points tempted like as we are, **yet without sin**. [16]Let us therefore come boldly unto the throne of grace, that we may obtain mercy, and find grace to help in time of need.*

Hebrews 2: 17-18: [17]Wherefore in all things 'he-owed' to be made like unto his brothers, that he might be a merciful and faithful High Priest in things pertaining to God, to make reconciliation for the sins of the people. [18]For in that he himself has 'emotion' being tempted, he is able to 'help' them that are tempted.

Mortals of Eternity

*Jude 1:6-7a: [6]And the angels which kept not their first estate, but left their own **habitation,** he hath reserved in everlasting chains under darkness unto the judgment of the great day. [7]**Even as Sodom and Gomorrah ....**

*Genesis 6:4: There were **giants (or, fallen ones)** in the earth in those days; and also, after that, when the sons of God came in unto the daughters of men, and they 'birth' to them, the same **mighty men** which 'from-eternity,' 'mortals' of 'the name.'*

*2 Corinthians 5:1: For we know that if our earthly **house** of this tabernacle were dissolved, we have a building of God, **a house not made with hands, eternal in the heavens.**

The sons of God were also a priestly group of "mortals of eternity," or **"mortals of the concealed"** (per Strong's

Concordance). This statement may seem contradictory. That is, they are "mortals" and yet "eternals;" they are mortals, yet of the concealed eternity. They apparently had the ability to be mortals [(migrate to the earth dimensions, temporarily (Genesis 14:18), or migrate as mortals permanently Genesis 6:4)]; yet they could also migrate to the eternal permanently, as well (Hebrews 7:3, Job 1:6; 2:1). They were also 'mortal' in the sense they apparently could procreate with the "daughters of 'the-Adam'" (Genesis 6:4). With that said, here are the Scriptures that can clarify the apparent contradiction between mortals, yet eternals and show .that sons of God are also called angels.

With regards to these eternal mortals, the New Testament speaks of angels (messengers) who left their "**own 'house'**" (Jude 1:6); a type of "house" the apostle Paul defined as an **eternal body, "house which is from heaven" and "not made with hands"** (2 Corinthians 5:2). These angels (messengers) or these **sons of God** with mortal-eternal bodies left their house (bodies) of heaven, permanently, to practice things in earth "even as Sodom and Gomorrah" (Jude 1:6-7, Genesis 6:4).

With that said, remember, Melchizedek was "made **like the Son of God" (Hebrews 7:3);** thus, where in the scriptures does "son(s) of God" or "like the Son of God" is equated to angel(s). The answer is **Daniel 3:25**, where "the form of the forth is **like the Son of God"** is later called an **"angel"** in **Daniel 3:28.** In other words, these angels apparently had eternal bodies that are human-like (sons of God); **yet not compatible** to procreate with **"the daughters of the-Adam"** as they tragically did.

In contrast, Melchizedek and His order of sons that remained faithful to the Lord God, were migrated to heaven (Hebrews 7:3). It follows that the sons of God of the New Covenant, who are under Jesus, the Son of the Living God, Jesus our Melchizedek, are "to be careful to maintain good work" and not become sons who defect from the living God.

Priest-Work

Hebrews 5:5; 6:.[5]*So also* **Christ** *glorified not himself to be made a High Priest; but He that said to him, ...***You are a priest forever after the order of Melchizedek** *.*

1 Peter 2:5: You also, as **'living' stones,** *are built up a spiritual house,* **a holy priesthood,** *to offer up* **spiritual sacrifices,** *acceptable to God by Jesus Christ.*

1 Peter 2:9: But you are a chosen generation, **a royal priesthood,** *a holy nation, a* **'purchased'** *people; that you should show forth the praises of him who has called you out of darkness into his marvelous light.*

Jesus is our High Priest; and like Aaron who had sons who were also priests, Jesus has brothers who are priest under Him. Peter stated that we are "a holy priesthood;" we are "a royal priesthood," or a "'kingly' priesthood." One of God's intents is to have a kingdom of priests (Exodus 19:6). So, we are a holy and royal priesthood.

Most believers confess that they are priests, however, most believers do not really know the function of New Testament priesthood. As priest unto God, one of our functions is to "offer up **spiritual sacrifices,** acceptable to God by Jesus Christ." "Spiritual" is defined as "things of the spirit." Hence, these spiritual sacrifices relate to the Spirit of God, and the spirit of man, the hidden man of the heart.

Spiritual Sacrifice

As the priest in the Old Testament offered up the sacrifices of animals, we are to offer up spiritual sacrifices to God. Some spiritual sacrifices are as follows:

1. Romans 12:1, Believer should present their bodies a living sacrifice to God, a **"logical** sacred-service."
   a. We present our bodies a living sacrifice by forsaking our life (desires), giving our bodies to teaching His Word, traveling to do God's work, evangelizing, sleeplessness, watching, fasting, marriage-sex, only; study the scripture for 8 hours per day, sit to write a book for hours upon hours, praying consistently, etc.
2. Hebrews 13:15, the sacrifice of praise, through all things.
   a. We are to give God the "sacrifice of praise and thanksgiving 'through all things,'" as we are to also give Him thanks "in everything" (1 Thessalonians 5:18).
3. Hebrews 13:16, the spiritual sacrifice of doing-good
   a. This is self-explanatory. Let us do good things and not bad things.
4. Hebrews 13:16, the spiritual sacrifice of sharing
   a. Sharing is part of the call of all believers. We are to offer spiritual sacrifice by sharing what we have with others (Galatians 6:6, Philippian 4:16-18).
5. Psalms 141:2, lifting our hands to God is as the evening sacrifice.
   a. The lifting of the hands is a spiritual sacrifice equal to the evening sacrifice. Lifting the hand also means thanksgiving. Paul declared that we are to pray and lift holy hands everywhere, not just in Church (1 Timothy 2:8)
6. Psalms 51:17, the spiritual sacrifices of a broken spirit and a contrite (lit., to collapse, crouch) heart
   a. The sacrifices that God desires are the spiritual sacrifices of a contrite hearts. He desires a broken spirts, not haughty spirits. That is, we are to fall on the Rock and be broken before the Lord Jesus (Luke 20:18).

Preaching the Gospel

Romans 15:15-16: *[15]Nevertheless, brethren, I have written the more boldly to you in some sort, as putting you in mind, because of the grace that is given to me of God, [16]That I should be the **'people-worker'** of Jesus Christ to the **'nations,'** **'priest-working'** the gospel of God, that the **offering up** of the **'nations'** might be acceptable, **being sanctified by the Holy 'Spirit.'***

In the reference above, Paul used language related to the priesthood in reference to evangelizing the nations. Like a priest who offer up sacrifices to God, apostles spiritually offer up the nations to God, after the nations are sanctified by the Holy Spirit. In addition, Paul defined the ministering of the gospel to the nations, as **"'priest-working' the gospel of God."** In Romans 15:20, he further defined the "priest-work" as "evangelizing" the nations.

Thus, one of the functions of being a priest is to preach the gospel to the nations. Saying it another way, when a believer preaches the gospel to whoever, that believer is doing the "priest-work."

"That Within the Veil"

As one studies the Scriptures in detail, the Spirit of the Lord will reveal that the function of the royal priesthood is also to function as a high priest. That is, the typology in Hebrews 9, and Hebrews, 10, referencing the work of the high priest on the Day of Atonement, represents Jesus, our Apostle, and High Priests; and it also represent all believers doing the same work as the corporate 'high priest, through or Great High Priest, Jesus Christ.

That is, through our Great High Priest, Jesus Christ, we can now enter the Holy of Holies by the blood of the Lamb of God. In the Old Testament, only the high priest was allowed into **"the second,"** the Holy of Holies with the blood of the sacrifice. In the

New Testament through Jesus Christ, all believers can enter "the second," the Holy of Holies by the blood of the Lamb.

*Hebrews 9:6-8: ⁶Now when these things were thus ordained, the priests went always into the first tabernacle, accomplishing the service of God. ⁷But **into the second** went **the high priest alone** once every year, not without blood, which he offered for himself, and for the errors of the people: ⁸The Holy 'Spirit' this signifying, that the **way** into the 'Holiest' was not yet made manifest, while as the first tabernacle was yet standing.*

Hebrews 10:19-20: ¹⁹Having therefore, brothers, boldness 'into the entrance' 'of-the' Holiest 'in' the blood of Jesus, ²⁰By a 'freshly-slain-sacrifice,' and living way, which he hath 'initiated' for us, through the veil, that is to say, his flesh

Pursuant to the Scriptures that was just read, it is clear the saints of the living God also have a high priest function in the Holy of Holies. Through Jesus' torn flesh on the cross (a symbol of the torn veil opening the way into the Holy of Holies), we can now enter the Holiest and speak with God in the Holy of Holies, in and through the sanctification of the eternal Spirit and the blood of Jesus.

Through Jesus we also have the priest-work of personifying **"that"** within the veil, or **"that"** which is in the Holy of Holies. This **"that"** is directly related to the Melchizedek's ministry.

*Hebrews 6:17-20: ¹⁷Wherein God, willing more abundantly to show to the heirs of promise the immutability of his counsel, confirmed it by an oath: ¹⁸That by two immutable things, in which it was impossible for God to lie, we might have a strong consolation, who have fled for refuge to lay hold upon the hope set before us: ¹⁹Which we have as an anchor of the soul, both sure and steadfast, and which enters into **that** within the veil; ²⁰Where the forerunner is for us entered, **Jesus,** made an **high priest 'into the age'** after the **order of Melchizedek.***

Thus, we see God made an oath (which cannot be broken), to confirm the promise and His plan for His heirs. These promises and His oath concerning the promises is our "hope" in Jesus; and this hope is related to "that" inside Holy of Holies, behind the veil where Jesus, our Forerunner, have entered. Note "within the veil" is defined as Jesus forerunning "into the age;" and within that veil, or "in the age" are vessels of ministry called **"that."**

So, the question must be asked, what is "that?" "That" to me speaks of "that" items that are behind the veil. The most prominent vessel within the veil is the Ark of the Covenant.

And most of "that" items were **within** the Ark of the Covenant, and **on** the Ark of the Covenant; except for the "golden censor." These items represent the work of Jesus, our High Priest, and the work of His priesthood that is to be personified through His Church.

Hebrews 9:1-5: ¹Then verily the first also had ordinances of divine service, and a worldly sanctuary. ²For there was a tabernacle made; the first, 'in which' was the candlestick, and the table, and the shewbread; which is called the sanctuary. ³And ***after the second veil,*** *the tabernacle which is called the 'Holies of the Holies;' ⁴Which had the* ***golden censer,*** *and* ***the ark of the covenant*** *'covered-about every-place' with gold, 'in which' was the* ***golden pot that had manna,*** *and* ***Aaron's rod*** *that budded, and the* ***tables of the covenant;*** *⁵And over it* ***the cherubs of glory*** *shadowing* ***the Mercy-seat;*** *of which we cannot now speak particularly.*

Hers is the itemized list of "that" within the veil for simplicity:

1. The gold censer
2. The Ark of the Covenant covered with gold
   a. The gold pot with mana placed in the Ark
   b. Aaron's rod that budded placed in the Ark
   c. The Tables of the Covenant placed in the Ark

d. The Cherubs joined to the Mercy-seat on the Ark

Gold Censer:

1. **The gold censer points to the priest-work of prayer.**
    a. "Censer" is the Greek word "thumiaterion" a utensil used for "incense burning." It is used in the Septuagint (LXX) in 2 Chronicle 26:19 relating to king Uzziah and Ezekiel 8:1). The root "thumiao" is used in Luke 1:9, when Zachariah was burning incense in the temple (the Holies of Holies). The base root also means "sacrifice." Also, Josephus, a Jewish historian, translated "thumiaterion" as the Altar of Incense

*Psalms 141:2: Let my **prayer** be set forth before you as **incense** ....*

*Revelation 5:8: And when he had taken the book, the four beasts and 'twenty-four' elders fell before the Lamb, having every one of them harps, and gold 'bowls' full of **'incense,' which are the prayers of saints.***

*Hebrews 7:22-23: [22]By so much was **Jesus** made a surety of a better Testament. [23]And they truly were many priests because they were not suffered to continue by reason of death: [24]But this, because He 'remains into the age,' has an 'unviolated' priesthood. [25]Wherefore he is able also to save them into the every-finish' that come unto God by him, **seeing he always lives 'into the' intercession 'over' them.***

Jesus said to His disciples, "'it-is-binding, they,' **always pray, and** not to faint" (see Luke 18:1).

Paul said, "through every prayer and petition, **pray in every season,** in Spirit" (see Ephesians 6:18).

Ark of the Covenant:

2. **The Ark of the Covenant points to the priest-work Jesus exemplified in His Covenant by sacrifice that is to be fulfilled in the people of God.**

The Ark of the Covenant represents Jesus. It is also worthy to note that the last place the "Ark" was seen is in heaven (Revelation 11:19). Did God translate the Ark of the Covenant to the temple in heaven?

In this section, my focus will be the word "covenant." Strong's Concordance defines covenant, as cutting flesh into to two (2) pieces and then walking between the pieces. This is seen in God's covenant with Abraham in Genesis

Genesis 15: 7-10, NAS: ⁷And He said to him, "I am the LORD who brought you out of Ur of the Chaldeans, to give you this land to possess it." ⁸He said, "O Lord GOD, how may I know that I will possess it?" ⁹So He said to him, "Bring Me a three year old heifer, and a three year old female goat, and a three year old ram, and a turtledove, and a young pigeon." ¹⁰Then he brought all these to Him and **cut them in two and** *laid each half opposite the other; but he did not cut the birds .... ¹⁷It came about when the sun had set, that it was very dark, and behold, there appeared a* **smoking oven and a flaming torch** *which* **passed between these pieces.**

This picture is also seen in the crucifixion of Christ. Jesus Christ, was cut in the flesh (whipped, nailed, pierced with a spear, punctured with thorns). In addition, Jesus was placed between the **two** bad-actors, who were also nailed to crosses and their bones broken. Thus, Jesus' crucifixion **between** the two thieves is a picture of God's everlasting covenant with those who accept Jesus Christ as the Son of God, the Christ!

Yet, there is more to the word Covenant that also testify of Jesus, the Son of God, crucified. The Hebrew word for **"covenant"** is **BRYTh (ברית) or brith.**

The first two letter of BRYTh is **BR (בר)**. **"BaR"** is defined as "son," "heir," "wheat;" and as we discussed earlier, this is exemplified when Jesus addressed Peter as "Simon **Bar** Jonah," meaning Simon, **son** of Jonah.

In addition, whenever the Hebrew letter "yad" or "yud" (י) is used at the end of a word, "yud" can be translated as "my." Tav (ת) means mark, sign, cross, covenant. Thus, the Hebrew pictograph for "covenant" is my (God's)-son-crucified, or the cross (of) my-son. Yes, Jesus is the Covenant. He is the Ark of the covenant. Jesus is the Ark of my (God's)-son-crucified!

A simple application of the Ark is that it represents a coffin and a place of resurrection. In Genesis 50:26, Joseph was embalmed and placed in an "ark;" and His bones kept there until the Exodus (Genesis 50:25-26, Exodus 13:19). With respect to resurrection, the Ark is the location of Aaron's stripped rod that rebloomed before the Lord presence (Numbers 17). Therefore, Aaron's rod represents the resurrection (blossoming) of Jesus Christ after His death (being stripped of life).

Thus, the Ark of the Covenant with respect to pries-work represents the work of Jesus, our High Priest who was crucified for us; raised from the dead; he presented His blood to the heavenly Father in the heavens; and thus, became our propitiation, our atoning Mercy-Seat. Part of our priest-work is to distribute this truth to the nations that they may believe on Jesus and be also atoned for.

Gold Pot with Mana:

"Pot" is translated from the Greek word "stamnos." One can hear the English word "stamina" in the word "stamnos." The root meaning for "stamnos" means to stand, or stationary. The pot held the "mana," literal bread from heaven, also called angels' food. We also learn earlier from John 6, that Jesus's body is the mana from heaven; and Jesus' "rhema" (words from a living voice) also represents mana. It must also be noted that on the sixth (6th) day, the Israelites could eat double portion, because no mana was available on the Sabbath day. This, principle is true for this sixth thousand year-day. There is double the revelation of Jesus Christ, in the evening of this current age!

So, let us put this all together:

Due to the priest-work being demanding, it requires stamina; and thus, mana from heaven must be eaten daily. Also, we are at the closing of the sixth thousand years from the first Adam, therefore, God will be distributing double portion of mana (revelation knowledge concerning Jesus) to sustain His priests in their priest-work.

Aaron's Rod that Blossomed:

Aaron's almond rod "in" the Ark also points to Jesus who is the firstfruit of all to be raised from the dead; yet Aaron's almond rod also points to the "firstfruit Christ" and the firstfruit "in" Christ to be raised ("budded") from the dead during the "seventh trumpet."

It is very significant that Aaron's rod was an almond rod. The Hebrew definitions for **almond** are wakeful, **sleeplessness,** watcher, hastener, alert, earliest to ripe, etc. The Scripture equates "sleep" to death (1 Thessalonians 4:16-17). Therefore, the almond being defined as the "sleeplessness" points to "watching's," and "deathlessness." Hence, the almond tree is also a symbol of resurrection, and watching in prayer.

The almond was the "first" of the fruit trees to "bud" during the "winter" (a symbol of tribulation) seasons. In Numbers 17, when Moses and Aaron's appointments as leaders (first among equals), were questioned, it was Aaron's rod, among the twelve

(12) rods, that God caused to blossom as a sign that the tribe of Levi was the chosen corporate leader of God. Again, Aaron's rod was the first **and the only** rod to blossom among the twelve rods that were stripped and placed before God; and it **"yielded almonds."**

Next, we must also understand that Aaron, himself, also points to the Ark being "revealed" (opened) in order that the blossoming almonds may be seen. This truth can be seen in the **hieroglyphics of Aaron's name.** Aaron's pictographic name may be interpreted to have various meanings. Aaron's pictographic name is a symbol of Jesus' resurrection as the greater Aaron. Aaron's name also pictorially means the Ark revealed.

In other words, Aaron's high priestly duty is a narrative of what the Ark represents. Saying it another way, the Ark represents Jesus, our Greater Aaron, or Jesus our Melchizedek functioning as our High Priest in the Holies of Holies. The Ark also represents those who will be reigning-priests (king-priests) of God, who will be ruling **with** Christ, our High Priest, during the seventh (7th) millennium.

With that said, let us look at the meanings of Aaron's name before, I give the pictographic understanding of Aaron's name.

Aaron's name is defined as: teacher, lofty, mountain of strength, mountaineer, enlightener (Hitchcock, Jerome, Gesenius, etc.). However, the Hebrew word picture for Aaron's name is very important to Lord's the priest-work.

The same Hebrew letters used in the spelling of **"Aaron"** are used in the spelling for the **"Ark."** The basic Hebrew for Aaron is transliterated as **AHRN (אהרן).** The transliteration of the Hebrew word for **Ark** is **ARN (ארן).**

The difference between the two words is that there is an "H" inserted in Aaron's name–**AHRN.** The pictographic idea of the Hebrew letter **"H" (ה)** is the picture of an **open window, or an** opening, to behold, breath, and "hey" (revealed to attract attention). When this Hebrew letter "H" is used at the end of a Hebrew word, it makes that word feminine.

However, when this letter **"H" (ה)** is used in the middle of a word, it means **to reveal,** to reveal the heart, to behold, and to look.

Thus "Aaron's" name is a picture of **"the Ark revealed;"** or his name pictures **"the revealed Ark;"** or Aaron's work as high priest **reveals** what the **Ark** represents. To make this simple, Aaron's name is a symbol of the heart of Jesus revealed, as our merciful High Priest who can understand our suffering, measure our sufferings; and comfort us through the Comforter. The priest-work of the order of Melchizedek is to evangelize this truth of Jesus' covenant (God's Son crucified for us) to the nations. Finally, the almond represents God's words of judgment in the mouth of His messengers that will be fulfilled speedily at the completion of this age, and during the age to come (see Jeremiah 1:11-12 w/Numbers 17:1-9).

The Tables of the Covenant

The tables of the covenant are the Ten "Sayings," also known as the Law. And note they are the "covenant" principles! "Table" is translated from the Greek word "plakes." In this word, "plaque" can be seen. The word "plakes" is also transliterated as "flat" surface like a plate or a tablet. I have already covered "covenant" under the subtitle "Ark of the Covenant." The Tables of the Covenant are summarized as such in Deuteronomy 5:6-21 and Exodus 20:1-17:

1. You shall have no other god before the LORD God.
   a. The LORD God is Jesus' God and Father
2. You shall not make any 'carved-idol' to bow down to them.
   a. God said that those who worship idols hate Him (Exodus 20:5 w/Exodus 20:3-5).

3. You shall not take the name of the LORD your God in vain.
   a. God name is not to be used in uselessness
4. Remember the Sabbath
   a. The Sabbath is now a Person—Jesus (Hebrews 4)
5. Honor your mother and father
   a. The is first commandment with a promise, long life.
6. You shall not murder
   a. No shedding of human blood is acceptable according to Genesis 9.
   b. However, we can bring healing to veterans who shed blood in the heat of war as opposed to cold blooded murder (1 Kings 2:5). In Genesis 14:19, after Abram returned from war, Melchizedek ministered communion, and blessings to Abram.
7. You shall not commit adultery
   a. The Hebrew pictograph shows that adultery is linked to anger related to posterity.
8. You shall not steal
   a. Compare Revelation 9:21 with Revelation 9:13-21
9. You shall not bear false witness against your neighbor
   a. False witnesses killed the Messiah and fruits (1 Kings 21)
10. You shall not covet
   a. Do not covet your neighbor's wife, house, field, servants, animals, or anything that belongs to your neighbor

With that said, the Law of God (Ten Sayings), the table of the covenant has been placed in us through the New Covenant.

Hebrews 10:16-17: *[16]This is the covenant that I will make with them after those days, saith the Lord, I will put **my laws** into their **hearts,** and in their **minds** will I **write them;** [17]And their sins and 'lawlessness' will I remember no more.*

In the Old Covenant, God wrote the ten laws upon stones. In the New Covenant, God writes His laws upon our hearts and minds. And there is additional promise in this New Covenant; the promise that the Father will not remember our sins and lawlessness, once we ask Him for forgiveness of sins!

The Cherubs joined to the Mercy-seat on the Ark

The Cherubs joined to the Mercy-Seat has many layers of truth. The intent of the section is only to give simple, meaningful understanding.

1. The two cherubs, joined to the Mercy-seat, with the flat surface of the Mercy-Seat between them is a picture of the flat area in tomb where Jesus was laid with two angels at the two ends after His resurrection. That is, the Mercy-Seat represents the resurrection of Jesus, and now the two angels (cherubs) must declare His resurrection to the "Mary" (bitter people, yet believers in Jesus) of this age. They are to show the power of His resurrection.

John 20:11-14: *[11]But **Mary** stood without at the sepulcher weeping: and as she wept, she stooped down, and looked into the sepulcher, [12]And saw **two angels** in white sitting, the **one at the head,** and **the other at the feet,** where the **body of Jesus** had lain. [13]And they say unto her, Woman, why 'are you weeping'? She says to them, because they have taken away my Lord, and I know not where they have laid him. [14]And when she had thus said, she turned herself back, **and saw Jesus standing,** and knew not that it was Jesus.*

2. The two cherubs are symbolic of the Two Witnesses in Revelation 11.
    a. The witness of the candlestick, the Church, (Revelation 1:20 with Revelation 11:3-4)
    b. The witness of the two olive trees, the Church, made up of Jews and Gentiles (Revelation 11:3-4 with Romans 11:11-24)
    c. The witness of the two olive trees, "the sons of fresh oil, who supply the gold oil to the candlestick, Jesus' Church, or the sons of the noon, or the sons of the light, or the sons of the window (Revelation 11:3-4 with Zechariah 4)
    d. The witness of the two prophets in earthly Jerusalem, **"where"** our Lord was crucified (Revelation 11:3-4; 7-8; 10-11).
    e. The witness of the two corporate prophets testifying of Jesus, in Babylon, "wherever" our Lord was crucified, "spiritually called Sodom and Egypt" (Revelation 11:3-4; 7-8; 10-11). Note: Practicing sodomy, as Sodom did, and withstanding God in the manner Jannes and Jambres withstood Moses, is the same as crucifying the Lord again (2 Timothy 3:8, Exodus 7, Genesis 19, Hebrews 6:4-6; with Revelation 11:7-10).

Thus, the priest-work of the Cherubs is through "great power" give witness of the resurrection of Jesus; supply gold oil to the wise virgins, testify against mystery Babylon, and so on.

3. The Mercy-Seat represents the atonement we received through Jesus Christ. In fact, John sated that Jesus is our Mercy-Seat.

*1 John 2:1-2: ¹My little children, these things write I to you, that you sin not. And if any man sin, we have an advocate with the Father, Jesus Christ the righteous: ²And **He is the Propitiation (or*** *lit., **Mercy-Seat**) for our sins: and not for ours only, but also for the whole world.*

Thus, "that" within the veil that pertains to the Mercy-Seat represents Jesus' as our Propitiator. Yes, part of Jesus' High Priest-work is that He is a merciful High Priest.

*Hebrews 2:17-18: [17]Wherefore in all things it 'He-owed' to be made like his brothers, that he might be a merciful and faithful high priest in things pertaining to God, **'into the propitiating'** (or **Mercy-Seat**) for the sins of the people. [18]For in that he himself has suffered-**'emotions'** being **'probed-tempted,'** he is able to 'help' them that are **'probe-tempted.'***

In closing of this section, "Mercy-Seat, (propitiation or propitiator) is from the root word transliterated as "cheerful." It is associated with the Greek word "hilaros." That is, Paul declares that those who are gifted with the priest-work of showing mercy, must do it "cheerfully." Thus, believe it, God shows mercy cheerfully and hilariously. This priest-work of showing mercy cheerfully is part of the Melchizedek order of priesthood.

*Romans 12:6a; 8d: [6]Having then **gifts differing according to the grace** that is given to us ....[8]... he that shows mercy, with **cheerfulness**.*

Be encouraged! Live a cheerful life, God has forgiven us through Jesus!

Righteousness-Peace-Life

*Hebrews 7:1-3: [1]For this Melchizedek, king of Salem, priest of the most high God, ... first being by interpretation **King of righteousness,** and after that also King of Salem, which is, **King of peace;** [3]... having neither beginning of days, nor end of life; but made like unto the Son of God; **abides a priest continually.***

*Romans 14:17: For the **kingdom of God** is not meat and drink; but **righteousness,** and **peace,** and **joy** in the Holy 'Spirit.'*

*Acts 2:28: You have made known to me the **ways of life;** You shall make me **full of joy** with Your countenance.*

Melchizedek's priesthood is demonstrated in the kingdom of God as a threefold king-priest service unto God and mankind. And according to Proverbs, the heavenly Father speaks in three-fold things; In addition, maturity in Christ can be measured in threes. It follows, Jesus' Melchizedek order and His kingly priests can be understood in threefold application.

*Proverbs 22:20: Have not I written to you **excellent** things in counsels and knowledge?*

1. "Written" can be applied to God's written Word (The Holy Bible)

2. "Excellent things" is the Hebrew word shaliysh (sha-leesh'), or shilshowm (shil-shome')
   a. "shalish means "a triple, three parts (Strong's #7991)
   b. Or shilshowm (shil-shome') means treble, three-fold, triplicate—three copies or examples (Strong's #8027, #8032)

Here are some examples of threefold things.

Threefold Things to Maturity		
1	2	3
Children	Young Men	Fathers
Common Faith	Great Faith	God's Faith (Mature Faith)
Common Salvation	Great Salvation	Eternal Salvation
Faith	Hope	Love
Spirit	Soul	Body
Seal of Circumcision without Hands	Seal of the Spirit	Seal in the Forehead (Mind)
Power	Great Power	Eternal, Creative or Mature Power
Righteousness	Peace	No end of life/Joy

Melchizedek's three-fold King-Priest Service consists of "righteousness," "peace" and "no end of life." *[1]For this Melchizedek, king of Salem, priest of the most high God, ... first being by interpretation **King of righteousness**, and after that also King of Salem, which is, **King of peace**; [3]Without father, without mother, without descent, having neither beginning of days, nor **end of life**; but **made like unto the Son of God; abides a priest continually** (Hebrews 7:1-3).*

1. Melchizedek—King of Righteous-togetherness, Melek (King) and Zedek (Righteousness)
2. King of Salam—King of Peace (Salem means "peace")
3. King of Life—like the Son of God, Melchizedek had "no end of life;" and he "abides a priest continually"

In Romans 14: 17, we also see similarity to Melchizedek. Except, in Romans, the threefold list is **"righteousness, peace and joy."** So, as we look at the threefold things of Melchizedek, a question that we explore is, **does joy equals life?**

*Romans 14:17: For the kingdom of God is not meat and drink; but **righteousness**, and **peace**, and **joy** in the Holy 'Spirit.'*

Melchizedek	Kingdom of God
Righteousness	Righteousness
Peace	Peace
No end of life	Joy

King of Righteousness

*Hebrews 7:1: For this **Melchizedek**, ... first being by interpretation **King of righteousness** ....*

*Romans 14:17: For the kingdom of God is not meat and drink; but **righteousness**, and peace, and joy in the Holy 'Spirit.'*

Paul plainly declared that the Kingdom of God is "in Holy Spirit." That is, God's kingdom of priest functions in the "Holy Spirit" and not outward garbs like we see today in the preferred clothing of the charismatic bishops and the robes of orthodox religion. With that said, the first of the three-phases of God's kingdom (the Melchizedek order) is righteousness.

Righteous-togetherness

"Righteousness" literally translates from the Greek as "righteous-togetherness" [dikaiosuné ("dikaio"-righteous and "sun"-togetherness, with)]. So, what is one of the meanings of "righteous-togetherness? Righteous-togetherness can mean that we are made righteous only "together" with Jesus and His righteousness.

Romans 3:21-22: ²¹ *But now the 'righteous-togetherness' of God without the law is manifested, being witnessed by the law and the prophets;* ²² *Even the **'righteous-togetherness' of God by faith of Jesus** Christ 'into' all and upon all them that believe: for there is no difference.*

It is through the faith of Jesus that we are made righteous **"together with"** Him. This righteous-togetherness of Jesus Christ is "into all, and upon all who believe" that Jesus is the Christ, the Son of the living God. Making this a little easier to understand, let us look at an analogy. If a person plays in the mud, say playing football, that person can get dirt/mud stain in his/her clothe if that person gets tackled in the mud. His or her interaction with the dirt/mud is rubbed off on his/her clothe. The same is true for Jesus' righteousness, in a clean way.

When we become "together" with Jesus, through faith in Jesus, Jesus' righteousness becomes our righteousness. That is, we become righteous; because we are joined to Jesus through faith. "**And because of him you are in Christ Jesus**, who became to us wisdom from God, **righteousness (lit., righteous-togetherness)** and sanctification and redemption (I Corinthians 1:30, ESV).

Ruling in Righteous-togetherness

Jesus is the King of Righteousness. Kings rule! Jesus' righteousness rules and causes us to rule in this life in righteousness. In other words, sin (missing God's mark for our lives) is exchanged for Jesus' righteousness. Through His grace, we are no longer considered unrighteous? How? Because, we have faith in Jesus Christ.

> *"For if, by the trespass of the one man, death reigned through that one man, how much more will those who receive an abundance of grace and of the **gift of***

righteousness (lit. righteous-togetherness) reign in life through the one man, Jesus Christ!" (Romans 1:17, Berean Study Bible)

Yes, through the Melchizedek King-Priest ministry of Jesus' righteousness, we can reign in life; and not allow death (swords, hunger, plagues, wild beasts, etc.) to reign over us. Jesus is King of Righteousness. He also makes war in righteousness on His enemies.

Revelation 19:11: And I saw heaven opened and behold a white horse; and he that sat upon him was called Faithful and True, and **in righteousness he doth judge and make war.**

Hebrews 10:12-14: [12] But this Man, after He had offered one sacrifice for sins forever, sat down on the right hand of God; [13] From henceforth **expecting until His enemies** *be made his footstool. [14] For by* **one offering** *He has perfected forever them that are sanctified.*

1 Corinthians 15:25-26: [25] For He must reign, until He has put all enemies under his feet. [26] The last enemy that shall be destroyed is **death.**

That is, anything that relates to death, through Jesus and because of Jesus, we overcome death. **"Death has no more dominion over us"** (Romans 6:9). Let us "walk by faith" of the Son of God, Jesus, and reign in life (living)!

Let **not** sickness, beasts (spiritual and literal), plagues, hunger, or death rule over us. Jesus is the King of the Righteous-togetherness. His gift of righteousness to us have freed us from all unrighteousness! "**If we confess our sins**, he is **faithful** and just to **forgive us** our sins and to **cleanse us** from **all unrighteousness**" (1 John 1:9, ESV).

Justification through Faith in Jesus

Melchizedek being King of Righteousness also speaks of "faith." Abraham is the father of faith and justification comes through faith. That is, righteousness in the Melchizedek's order is a result of faith. Jesus ratified justification by faith, through His faith unto death and resurrection; not by animal sacrifices. **God, the heavenly Father abolished animal sacrifice forever, through Jesus' one sacrifice.** With that said, please read the references below. It will show that men ought not to pursue animal sacrifices again or rebuilding a natural temple.

*⁴For it is **not possible** that the blood of bulls and of goats should take away sins. ⁵Wherefore when he cometh into the world, he saith, sacrifice and offering you willed not, but a Body hast you prepared me: ⁶In **burnt offerings and sacrifices for sin you have had no pleasure.** ⁷Then said I, Lo, I come (in the volume of the book it is written of me,) to do your will, O God. ⁸Above when he said, Sacrifice and offering and burnt offerings and offering for sin you 'willed' not, neither has pleasure therein; which are offered by the law; ⁹Then said He, Lo, I come to do your will, O God. He takes away the first, that he may establish the second. ¹⁰By the which will we are sanctified through the offering of the Body of Jesus Christ, **once** (Hebrews 10:4-10).*

*Jeremiah 7:22-23, NAS: ²²"**For I did not speak to your fathers, or command them in the day that I brought them out of the land of Egypt, concerning burnt offerings and sacrifices.** ²³"But this is what I commanded them, saying, '**Obey My voice,** and **I will be your God, and you will be My people;** and you will walk in all the way which I command you, that it may be well with you.'*

The apostle Paul also declares that the gospel of Jesus Christ, reveals the righteousness of God, which comes through faith in Jesus Christ.

*Romans 1:17, BLB: For in it the righteousness of God is revealed from faith to faith, as it has been written: **"And the righteous will live by faith."***

*Genesis 15:6: And [Abram] **believed** in the LORD; and he counted it to him for righteousness.*

Thus, the Melchizedek's order of priests are people of faith, who walk with God by faith; and they live by faith!

*2 Corinthians 5:7: For we **walk by faith**, not by sight.*

*Galatians 3:11: And it is clear that no one is justified before God by the law, because **"The righteous will live by faith."***

King of Peace

*Hebrews 7:1-2: For this Melchizedek, **king of Salem,** ... which is, **King of peace.***

*Romans 14:17: For the kingdom of God is not meat and drink; but righteousness, and **peace**, and joy in the Holy 'Spirit.'*

In this section, I will first establish some principles with regards to peace as it relates to God, Jesus, Melchizedek, and Jerusalem.

Peace is defined as "freedom from disturbance; tranquility." The classical Greek definition conform more to the Hebrew definition of peace. **Peace is the Greek word eirḗnē (from eirō, "to join, tie together into a whole"); "properly, wholeness, i.e., when all essential parts are joined together; peace (God's gift of wholeness)."** The Hebrew word "Salem" means peace, complete, safe, friendly, whole.

Thus, God's idea of a priesthood that walks in peace is directly related to the essential members of the body of Christ being joined functioning as one body of priests, the "priest-togetherness."

King of Salem, King of Peace

When Melchizedek met Abram, Melchizedek was declared to be king of Salam. Notice, he was not king of Jerusalem, but king of Salam. At the time, Melchizedek, met Abram, earthly, Jerusalem was not introduced in the Holy Writ. Melchizedek was the king of the heavenly Salem, where there was only one Salem. Thus, he was king of peace, king of friendliness, king of safety, king of wholeness, king of completion. Does these descriptions sound like the work of our Messiah, Jesus Christ? Yes, Jesus, has completed us forever. Jesus calls us friends. Jesus is our wholeness. Jesus is our salvation (safety)!

Jerusalem (plural)

Jerusalem (Yruwshalaim or Yruwshalayim[2]) is "dual," and plural in the Hebrew. According to the apostle Paul, this means there are two (2) Jerusalem, "Jerusalem, above, and Jerusalem, which now is on earth.

Galatians 4:25-26: [25]For this Agar is mount Sinai in Arabia, and 'corresponds' to Jerusalem which now is, and is in 'slavery' with her children. [26]But Jerusalem which is above is free, which is the mother of us all.

When Salem and its King, Melchizedek, was introduced to Abram, it was introduced in "peace." When Jerusalem (dual) was introduced for the first time in Joshua 10, its king was introduced as an enemy of Gibeon and Joshua. Also, the king of earthly Jerusalem, Adonizedek, was the chief coordinator of the alliance of the kings against Joshua and the Jews.

Joshua 10:1-5; 7-8: [1]Now it came to pass, when Adonizedek king of Jerusalem had heard how Joshua had taken Ai and had utterly destroyed it; as he had done to Jericho and her king, so he had done to Ai and her king; and how the inhabitants of Gibeon had

---

[2] Yruwshalayim (מירושלים) is found 2 Chronicles 25:1 and Esther 2:6

made peace with Israel and were among them .... ³Wherefore **Adonizedek king** *of* **Jerusalem** *sent unto Hoham king of Hebron, and unto Piram king of Jarmuth, and unto Japhia king of Lachish, and unto Debir king of Eglon, saying, ⁴Come up unto me, and help me .... ⁵Therefore the five kings of the Amorites,* **the king of Jerusalem,** *the king of Hebron, the king of Jarmuth, the king of Lachish, the king of Eglon ... encamped before Gibeon, and made war against it .... ⁷So Joshua ascended from Gilgal, he, and all the people of war with him, and all the mighty men of valor. ⁸And the LORD said unto Joshua, fear them not: for I have delivered them into your hand; there shall not a man of them stand before you.*

Without getting into too much detail, it can be clearly seen that "Adonizedek, is the king of Jerusalem. This same king made war with Gibeon and Joshua. Thus, he and his alliance of kings were enemies of the Jews. Additionally, it was at this juncture in God's history, Jerusalem (dual) is introduced. That is, since Melchizedek, did not die, he lives continually, Salem still existed. In addition, at that time, there was now a "dual" Salem (Jerusalem).

This "dual" Salem (Jerusalem) also has a king, "Adonizedek" lord-of righteousness, or sovereign of righteousness. First, one must note that this "Adonizedek" was not sovereign or related to the Sovereign God; because if he were, he would not have attacked Gibeon or Joshua. Thus, **like false apostles,** Adonizedek points to a duplicate priesthood, or a duplicate righteousness that attempts asserts sovereignty over God's people with their "own" standards of righteousness.

Romans 10:3: For being ignorant of the righteousness of God and seeking to establish the **own righteousness,** *they did not submit to the righteousness of God.*

Luke 18:9: To some who trusted in their **own righteousness** *and viewed others with contempt, He also told this parable ...*

Philippians 3:8-9: *⁸More than that, I count all things as loss compared to the surpassing excellence of knowing Christ Jesus my Lord, for whom I have lost all things. I consider them rubbish, that I may gain Christ. ⁹ and be found in Him, **not** having **my own righteousness** from the law, but that which is through faith in Christ, the righteousness from God on the basis of faith.*

2 Corinthians 11:11-15, BSB: *¹³For such men are false apostles, deceitful workers, masquerading as apostles of Christ. ¹⁴And no wonder, for Satan himself masquerades as an angel of light. ¹⁵It is not surprising, then, if his servants **masquerade as servants of righteousness.** Their end will correspond to **their actions.***

Jerusalem—Priest-Peace

Jesus declared that His disciples was a "city." He also said that this "city" (His disciples) were situated on the top of a mountain. Jerusalem is that City that represents the Church of Jesus.

Galatians 4:26: ***Jerusalem which is above is** free, which is the mother of us all.*

*Hebrews 12:22: But **you have come** to Mount Zion, and the city of the living God, **the heavenly Jerusalem,** and to myriads of angels.*

*Revelation 21:10: And he carried me away in the Spirit to a great and high mountain, and he showed me the holy city **Jerusalem, descending out of heaven** from God.*

*Matthew 5:14, Darby: 'You' are the light of the world: a **city** situated on the top of a **mountain** cannot be hid.*

*Revelation 21:2: I saw the holy city, the **new Jerusalem,** coming down out of heaven from God, prepared **as a bride** adorned for her husband.*

Again, Jesus declared that His disciples was a "city." He also said that this "city" (His disciples) were situated on the top of a mountain. In the book of Revelation, we also see that the holy city, Jerusalem was viewed from a high mountain. In the book of Hebrews, the author clearly states that the heavenly Jerusalem is in Mount Zion; and finally, Peter declared Zion to be a people, who were not a people; but now, they are God's royal priesthood. Saying it explicitly. Jerusalem is the Church of Jesus Christ. Jerusalem is Church, the Bride of Christ! If you can receive Jerusalem is the city for God's "'kingly' priesthood" who are according to the order of Melchizedek. Jerusalem is God's city where His priest can rest in God's peace

Jerusalem in the New Testament is translated from the Greek compound word "Hierusalem," "Hierosoluma." **"Hieros"** is a Greek word translated in the Bible as "temple (sanctuary)," "sacred," "holy" "ministering" and "priest." **"Salem"** means "peace" as previously stated. Therefore, Jerusalem in the New Testament can be translated as "Priest-Peace," Priest-Wholeness, Priest-Salvation, Priest-Safety, Priest-Friends, and so on. Let us have peace **"with"** God and walk in the peace **"of"** God.

Peace "of" God versus Peace "with" God

I learn a long time ago from Dr. Kelley Varner that there is a difference between peace **"with"** God and having the peace **"of"** God. We have peace with God once we accept Jesus Christ as the Son of the living God. That is, in our joining to Jesus, we become whole being justified through faith; and we can now seek to appropriate that wholeness as we walk with the Father by faith.

*Romans 5:1: Therefore, since we have been justified through faith, we have **peace with God** through our Lord Jesus Christ.*

God, who cannot lie, indicated in the reference above, that peace is directly related to Justification, through Jesus. Thus, if peace with God is missing in your life, then you may not be "whole" in justification. Through Jesus, at no cost to us, and no work on our part, His grace has rendered us righteous and innocent. Therefore, we can get rid of the turmoil of condemnation and any evil-emotion of feeling like you are always wrong in whatever choices you make. All believers have been recreated intrinsically-right!

The "peace **of** God" is a little higher than "peace **with** God." The peace **of** God is when we have God's peace" imparted to us, also through faith. It is the peace that has its origin in God, and thus, from God. It is a peace that overcome the Devil. It is peace of God that "umpires" and guards the heart and mind, with the understanding that "peace" is defined a wholeness with all the parts (members) joined.

*Philippians 4:7: And the **peace of God**, surpassing all understanding, will **guard your hearts and your minds** in Christ Jesus.*

*Colossians 3:15, Berean: And let the **peace of Christ 'arbitrate'** in your hearts, to which also you were called in one body. And be thankful.*

*Colossians 3:15, KJV: And let the **peace of God 'arbitrate'** in your hearts, to the which also you are called in one body; and be ye thankful.*

The layers of truth above is awesome. With regards to decision making, "the peace of Christ" is to be the arbitrator. That is, sometimes, in decision making, whether to do, or not do something; if there is no peace, then do not do it. The Peace of God is also linked to the body functioning as "one," which is part of the classical Greek definition of "peace." If you are unsettled in a decision, stand sill; because of a lack of peace.

"Let the peace of God 'arbitrate' in your hearts, to the which also <u>you are called in one body."</u> The peace that has its source in God acts as an "umpire." In addition, the peace of God, surpasses all understanding, and thus, guards our hearts and mind. That is, the peace that has its origin from God can give you God's peace in any trying situation, or decision making; and there is no logical explanation for this peace; because the peace we feel is beyond understanding, and beyond the understanding of those observing us.

The God of Peace

Romans 16:20a: And in a short time, **the God of peace** *will* **crush Satan under your feet**. *The grace of our Lord Jesus Christ be with you.*

The verse above is very telling! God crushes Satan for us! Yes, God crushes Satan, "under [our] feet" through peace. And note, Paul stated that it is the "God of peace" who crushed Satan. That is, it is not "our" peace "with" God that crushes Satan under our feet; but it is the God **of** peace. In other words, God's desire is the wholeness of peace; and through His peace He will "swiftly" crush Satan, under of feet. The Melchizedek ministry is a ministry of peace, peace that sees our enemies crushed under our feet.

Ephesians 6:10-18, Berean: [10]*Finally, be strong in the Lord and in His mighty power.* [11]*Put on the full armor of God, so that you can make your stand against the devil's schemes.* [12]**For our struggle is not against flesh and blood, but against the rulers, against the authorities, against the powers of this world's darkness, and against the spiritual forces of evil in the heavenly realms**. [13]*Therefore take up the full armor of God, so that when the day of evil comes, you will be able to stand your ground, and having done everything, to stand.* [14]*Stand firm then, with the belt of truth buckled around your waist, with the breastplate of righteousness arrayed,* [15]**and with your feet fitted with the readiness of the gospel of peace**. [16]*In addition to all this, take up the shield of faith, with which you can extinguish all the flaming arrows of the evil one.* [17]*And take the helmet of salvation and the sword of the Spirit, which is the word of God.* [18]*Pray in the Spirit at all times, with every kind of prayer and petition. To this* *end, stay alert with all perseverance in your prayers for all the saints*

King of Life

---

*Hebrews 7:1-3: ¹For this Melchizedek, ...³Without father, without mother, without descent, having neither beginning of days, **nor end of life**; but made like unto the Son of God; **abides a priest continually.***

*Romans 14:17: For the kingdom of God is not meat and drink; but righteousness, and peace, and **joy** in the Holy 'Spirit.'*

Melchizedek threefold description is that of Righteousness, peace and "no end of life." Paul description of God's kingdom is that of righteousness, peace, and joy. It follows that "joy" seems to be a synonym of "life," or joy is directly related to life.

This can be seen in one of the Scriptures that discusses the "ways (plural) of life."

The Ways of Life

*Acts 2:28: You have made known to me the **ways of life**; You shall make me **full of joy** with Your countenance.*

Peter's quote above was taken from Psalms 16:11: In Psalm "ways" (plural) is translated as "path" (singular). Proverbs also speaks about the "path of life" that relates to chastisements through instructions. With that said, my intention is to focus on joy that relates to "life," and not necessarily the principles cited in Proverbs. So, let us unpack a meaning of Acts 2:28, in simplicity.

Since Peter stated that the "ways" of life is plural, it follows, there must be more than one component to "life" in his statement; and it appears to me that Peter does indeed provide at least two (2) ways of life (joy and God's presence). **The first way of life is**

God **"filling us with joy."** Thus, this goes well with Romans 14:17 relative to "joy," and the Melchizedek ministry relative to "life." That is, the ways of **life** are directly related to having **"joy."** Jesus was/is a joyful man!

Joy-Life

'Full of joy," as Peter cited, literally translate as "good-disposition," "well-disposition," "good-minded," or "well-minded." **The classical usage in ancient Greece is that of good-cheer, gladness, and joy.** That is, our disposition of joy is linked to the disposition of our inward thoughts. So how does God fill us with the "well-disposition" of joy and gladness, in our thoughts? God gives us joy through his **"presence,"** the second part of the ways of life. As Peter indicated, "[The Lord] shall make me **full of joy** with [His] **countenance" (lit., presence).**

Yes, spending time in God's presence fills us with joy, gladness, cheerfulness, good-disposition, etc. And, yes, joy results in life! Thus, these are two (2) of the ways (plural) of life—**Joy** through "good-disposition," and God's **presence** through worship, thanksgiving, prayer, doing His commandments, and so on.

Priest-Togetherness

One of the most difficult things for Christ's believers to express pragmatically is that we are one with Christ and the Father (John 17:21-23). When the Church understand our "togetherness" with Jesus Christ and the Father is one, the World will come to "believe" and "know" that God sent Jesus (John 17:21, 23). This concept can also be understood in the Melchizedek order in Jesus Christ. That is, we are "priest-together" with Jesus, our Great High Priest. However, before I briefly exegete the priest-togetherness, let us briefly discuss "the Great-togetherness," which will make it easier to understand the priest-togetherness.

The Great-togetherness

*Hebrews 8:1 Now of the things which we have spoken this is the sum: We have such a high priest, who is set on the right hand of the throne of **the Majesty** in the heavens;*

"Majesty" is a Greek compound word "megalosune" (mega and sun). It is used only three (3)[3] times in the Bible. "Mega" means great and large, and "sun" means "togetherness" or "with." Therefore, "majesty" in the reference above literally reads "Great-togetherness." So, the verse should read:

> *"Now of the things which we have spoken this is sum: We have such a High Priest, who is set "in" the right hand of **the throne** of the **"Great-togetherness"** in the heavens."*

Let us look at this in detail. In **"the Throne** of the Great-togetherness," God sits; in the same "Throne of the Great-togetherness," Jesus sits in God's right hand, according to the order of Melchizedek; and in the same "Throne of the Great-togetherness" is the Sevenfold Spirit of God is also before the

---

[3] Hebrews 1:3, Hebrews 8:1 and Jude 1:25

throne. As it is written: [4]John, to the seven churches in the province of Asia: Grace and peace to you from **Him who is and was and is to come,** and from **the seven Spirits** before His throne, [5]and **from Jesus Christ,** the faithful witness, the firstborn from the dead, and the ruler of the kings of the earth. (Revelation 1:4-5). This is the "Great-togetherness." All three as one, working together as one.

Revelation 5:1; 6, BSB: [1]Then I saw a scroll in the right hand of the **One seated on the throne.** *It had writing on both sides and was sealed with seven seals .... [6]Then I saw a* **Lamb** *who appeared to have been slain,* **standing in the center of the throne,** *encircled by the four living creatures and the elders.* **The Lamb had seven horns and seven eyes,** *which* **represent the seven Spirits of God** *sent out into all the earth.*

In the Great-togetherness, the heavenly Father sits on the throne; Jesus, the Lamb of God, who was slain for our sins, is also in the middle of the throne; and thirdly, the sevenfold Spirits of God functions in this Great-togetherness as the eyes of the Lamb of God!. God is the "Great King" of the "Great-togetherness;" Jesus is the Great Hight Priest of the Great-togetherness; and the "Eternal Spirit," is the Life-giver of the "Great-togetherness," and so on.

Priest-togetherness

Considering the Great-togetherness of God, the Father, God, the Son, and God the Spirit functioning as one, the "priest-togetherness" must also function **as one** with Jesus. That is, the Church of Jesus must work in unison. Priest-togetherness is also written in three (3) places in Scriptures as "hierosune" ["hiero" ("priest") and "sun" (togetherness)].

1. "Priest-togetherness" is mentioned relative to the Aaronic priesthood mandate to mature the people of God through legislating laws to the people. In this first

66

context, the emphasis is legislating tithing to the Aaronic order of priests (Hebrews 7:11 w/Hebrews 7:1-10).

2. "Priest-togetherness" is mentioned a second time, relative to the change of the law by establishing that the Melchizedek order is not inherited according "flesh" (race, ethnicity, color, nationality); but inherited through God's oath, according to "the power of 'un-loosed' life," (Hebrews 7:12 w/Hebrews 7:13-17; Hebrews 7:28).

3. "Priest-togetherness" is used the third time relative to the Melchizedek priesthood "remaining 'into the age';' and thus, "untransgressable" (Hebrews 7:24 w/Hebrews 7:23)

In simplistic explanation:

1. The Melchizedek priest-togetherness is made of King Jesus, and His "kingly priesthood," the Church of Jesus. In addition, the Melchizedek order legislate the laws of the New Covenant, the law of love, the law of faith, the mature law of freedom, and so on.

2. The Melchizedek priest-togetherness also relates to a kingly priesthood that has "endless life," or a life that cannot be loosed from us. In other words, the priest-togetherness applies to us now, in this life, and the priest-togetherness will continue "into the age" where Jesus now resides as the Great High Priest. Jesus will complete his work in us, even after we sleep in Him!

3. The Melchizedek order of the priest-togetherness is "untransgressable," or "inviolable." The terms or law of His priesthood cannot be broken, infringed upon, or dishonored; and Jesus will never violate any, or transgress against any. (It follows that we, his royal priesthood, also Has Jesus's inviolable nature.) Jesus priesthood will never be removed from us because He

made it "sure" in His "limbs" through the cross. He is remaining beside us forever, as He "always" performs His High priestly duty on our behalf interceding for us to the "every-finish."

"Into the Age"

*Hebrew 7:21: (For those priests were made without an oath; but this with an oath by Him that said to Him, the Lord swore and will not repent, You a priest **'into the age'** after the order of Melchizedek:*

*Hebrews 6:5, BSB: who have tasted the goodness of the word of God and the **powers of the coming age.***

*Luke 20:34-35: [34] And Jesus answering said to them, the **'sons'** of this **'age'** marry, and are given in marriage: [35] But they which shall be accounted worthy to obtain **that 'age,'** and the resurrection from the dead, neither marry, nor are given in marriage*

The Melchizedek order of priests' functions in a place called "into the age." That is, "the age" is a heavenly dimension, it is the heavenly Holy of Holies. And though "the age" will also be fulfilled as a literal age; a pragmatic application of "the age" is Jesus in His Church functioning as "that" inside the veil.

In addition, as the "candlestick" represents Jesus in the middle of His Church (Revelation 1:12-20), the table of showbread represents, Jesus, the Bread of God, among other things; so, the Ark of the Covenant, the Mercy-seat, the Pot with Mana, Aaron's rod, the Cherubs united with the Mercy-seat represents the function of Jesus as High Priest and His royal priesthood functioning as priest under Jesus.

With that said, and as I previously stated, "the age" is also a literal age of 1,000-year era of God's many ages. The ages of God can be viewed from different vantage point. God's ages can be looked at as seven prophetic days (one prophetic week of seven thousand-year periods). **Peter said, "one day with the Lord is as a thousand years; and a thousand years as one day."** Hence, as there are seven days in one week, there are seven thousand years in a week of the ages.

In this section, I will use the vantage point of three-fold things to define the ages, starting from Moses. That is, we can look at the ages based on the pattern of the "Tent of Set-time," God commissioned Moses to build.

The Law Age

There was the Law age, symbolized by the Outer Court of the Tabernacle Moses was commanded to build according to the pattern. This age of the Law lasted approximately 1,500 years. That is, by adding all the dimensions (perimeter) of the Tabernacle's Outer Court (100 + 100 + 50 + 50 = 300 cubits) and multiplying the total by the height of five cubits (300 cubits x 5 cubits = 1,500 cubits[2]), the total as indicated is fifteen hundred square cubits. The Law of Moses, including animal sacrifices, historically lasted approximately fifteen hundred (1,500) years, before Jesus Christ came and abolished animal sacrifice forever.

The Age of Grace

Then, there is the current age of Grace, which is to span approximately 2,000 years. This current age is symbolized by the Holy Place in the tabernacle that Moses built. The Holy Place was ten (10) cubits wide, twenty (20) cubits long, and ten (10) cubits high.

Again, using simple mathematics, 20 x 10 x 10 equals 2,000 cubits[3]. The Holy Place of the Tabernacle of the Congregation (or lit., "Tent of Set-time," "Tent of Meeting-time," etc.) shows that the Church has been in existence for approximately 2,000 years. That is, the age of the Law ended with Jesus, and Jesus then instituted the Age of Grace. The Age of Grace, as we know it, will only last for approximately 2,000 years. We are coming to the close of the second millennium from Jesus Christ's death, burial, and His powerful resurrection.

"The Age"

Then there is an age that the Bible calls "that age," or "the age to come." This "age" is sometimes used in the phrase "into the age." "Into the age" is sometimes translated as "for ever" in the King James Version, or "forever" in the more modern versions. This age is symbolized by the Holy of Holies, in the "Tent of Set-time" that Moses built. This age is to last approximately 1,000 years.

Jesus' Melchizedek Priesthood (His royal priesthood) is maturing into fulfilling the next admeasurements of the "Tent of Set-time" called the "the age about to be." In other words, the dimensions of the Holy of Holies along with its furniture(s) provides the pattern of the next 1,000 years, which Jesus called "that age."

The Holy of Holies dimensions were 10 Cubits x 10 Cubits x 10 Cubits; and when multiplied to find the volume, the dimensions total 1,000 cubits[3]. The volume of the Holiest of Holies is the same length as the millennium—1,000 years (Revelation 20:4-6).

Therefore, when Jesus entered the Holiest of Holies in the heavens, He effectively entered "the age," or "that age," which functions in all aspects of resurrection life, eternal power, eternal priesthood, and so on. "That age" was introduced to us through Jesus, expounded upon by Peter and Paul, and specified through Jesus to the beloved John in the book of the Revelation of Jesus Christ.

The Revelation of Jesus Christ, in the book of Revelation, is an unveiling of the Melchizedek priest-togetherness. In other word, the book of Revelation shows the Church representing the High Priest Jesus executing the Melchizedek order in the earth. Thus, in Revelation 20: 1-6, we see the resurrection phase of Jesus' "kingly' priesthood" who will rule **"with Christ"** in the age of the millennium, the same "age" that Jesus is currently seated in.

The Age of King-Priests

*1 Peter 2:9: But you are a chosen generation, a **royal priesthood**, a **holy** nation ....*

*Revelation 20:6: Blessed and **holy** is he that has part in the first resurrection: on such the second death has no 'authority,' but they shall be **priests of God and of Christ**, and shall **reign (or, kings)** with him a thousand years.*

"Royal priesthood," can be translated as "kingly priesthood." The word "reign," in the text above, is translated as "kings" in 1 Timothy 6:16, where Jesus is called the "King of **kings."** Therefore, Revelation 20:6c can be translated as: "but they shall be **priests** of God and Christ, and **'kings'** with Him a thousand years." These definitions (Peter's and John's) make it clear that the Father's intent is to have a "kingly priesthood," or "priest ... kings."

This truth compliments the Melchizedek priesthood of Jesus Christ. Melchizedek is a king! Melchizedek is a priest of the Highest God! Melchizedek is a king-priest. Jesus is the King. Jesus is the High Priest. Jesus is the Great Priest. Jesus is the first Melchizedek. It follows that Jesus' believers are also a "kingly priesthood;" and as "priests" we will be "kings" with Him in the millennium age!

Thus, "that age" which Jesus calls the era in which the **"worthy"** will be resurrected, is the continuation of the "excellent" ministry of the Melchizedek order. We will rule with Christ in His throne, as Christ is now ruling in His Father's throne!

With that said, and before I speak about the "power" of the age to come, I also want to show that even though the millennium is an age of resurrection and the age of the imprisonment of the "original serpent," generations of humanity will still continue in that age. Yes, humanity will be living longer as the days of trees yet birthing and dying will continue until Death and Hades is cast into the lake of fire after the resurrection of eternal judgment.

Generations of-the Age of-the Ages

Ephesians 3:20-21: [20]*Now to Him that is able to do exceedingly abundantly above all that we ask or think, according to the power that* **'energizes'** *in us,* [21]*Unto him, glory in the church by Christ Jesus* **'into all the generations of-the age of-the ages.'** *Amen.*

The phrase "into all the generations of-the age of-the ages" has many layers of truth.

1. There will be "generations" (plural) of "the age." That is, even though the first resurrection takes place at the beginning of the seventh millennium, some of the people of the nations will still reproduce and live on for that period.

2. "The age" is the age of the ages, which makes it significant of all the previous ages. It will be the Sabbath age, the age of resting in His power.

3. "The age" of the ages is the millennium age in which God's **"glory (or, esteem)** in the Church by Christ Jesus" will manifested through Jesus' Melchizedek order.

Thus, in "the age of the ages" there will be generations that will continue as mankind has reproduced since the first Adam, except without the deception of "the original serpent." In other words, after the first resurrection occurs, generations continue in "the age," and according to Isaiah sin will also continue. Therefore, the Melchizedek priesthood will continue to function, as priest of God and Christ, except at a higher level **with** **Christ**.

Power of the Age to Come

*Hebrews 6:5, BSB: who have tasted the goodness of the word of God and the **powers of the coming age.***

The age to come will be an age of power. Power is also translated as "miracles" in the New Testament. It will be an age in which the miraculous power of God will be manifested as Jesus manifested God's power on the Sabbaths. When Jesus came in the flesh approximately 2,000 years ago, He purposely worked on the Sabbaths days. As you read the books of Matthews, Mark, Luke, and John, it become evident that Jesus worked his miracles on Saturdays (the Sabbath). Why the Sabbath? It appears to me that there are at least three (3) reasons Jesus manifest His power on the Sabbath.

1. Jesus said that His Father, God, has been working in the Sabbath, so He also works on the Sabbath. That is, the heavenly Father has been using His power to heal mankind, since Adam's first sin on the Sabbath.

2. Jesus made it clear that it is okay to do good on the Sabbath; and Peter stated that Jesus "went about doing good, healing all who were under the 'dynasty' of the Devil"

3. Jesus exemplified to us on Saturdays (Sabbath days) what is to happen in the Sabbath millennium (the seventh one thousand-year counting from the first Adam).

In "the age to come" the royal priesthood will be walking in "mature power." That is, as Jesus healed on Saturdays, cast out demons on Saturdays, cleaned lepers on Saturdays, raised the dead on Saturdays, open blind eyes on Saturdays, preached the gospel on Saturdays, and so on; so likewise, those who has course in the first resurrection will be demonstrating God power as priest in that **Sabbath** millennium, according to the order of Melchizedek.

Melchizedek and War

Genesis 14:17-20: [17]*And the king of Sodom went out to meet [Abram] after his return from the slaughter of Chedorlaomer, and of the kings that were with him ....* [18]*And **Melchizedek king of Salem brought forth bread and wine: and he was the priest of the 'Highest' God.*** [19]*And he blessed him, and said, blessed be Abram of the 'Highest' God, possessor of heaven and earth:* [20]*And blessed be the **Highest God, which has delivered your enemies into your hand.** And he gave him tithes of all.*

Psalms 110:1-6: [1]*The LORD said to my Lord, sit you at my right hand, until I make **your enemies** your footstool.* [2]*The LORD shall send the rod of your strength out of Zion: **'dominate' you in the middle of thine enemies.*** [3]*Your people shall be willing in the day of your power, in the beauties of holiness from the womb of the morning: you have the dew of your youth.* [4]*The LORD has sworn, and will not repent, you are a priest forever after the order of Melchizedek.* [5]*The Lord at your right hand shall strike through kings in **the day of his wrath.*** [6]*He shall judge among the heathen, he shall fill the **places with the dead bodies;** he shall **wound** the heads over many countries.* [7]*He shall drink of the **brook (lit., river, or inheritance)** in the way: therefore, shall he lift-up the head.*

Hebrews 7:1-2,NASB: [1]*For this Melchizedek, king of Salem, priest of the Most High God, who met **Abraham as he was returning from the slaughter** of the kings **and blessed him.***

The first mention of Melchizedek in the book of Genes was after a war that Abraham fought and won. In addition, many were "slaughtered" at this war. After the war, Melchizedek blessed the Highest God who "has delivered [Abraham} **enemies into [Abraham's] hand"** So, it is apparent that Melchizedek introduced himself to Abraham after that war when Abraham defeated his enemies. Thus, we see the Melchizedek ministry is associated with war! Thus, Christians should also be involved in healing military men who experience war through the Melchizedek order.

In the second mention of Melchizedek in the book of Psalms, it also deals with defeating enemies, judging the nations through war, striking kings (related to the beast), the Lord filling the land with dead bodies, and wounding head over nations. This sounds like war, does it not? In Hebrews 7:1-2, Melchizedek also blessed Abraham after the slaughter of the kings. **This is diametrically different from our concept of priests.**

Melchizedek is a king; so, he had to deal with war. The same is true for King Jesus. He also makes war in righteousness. "And I saw heaven opened, and behold a white horse; and he that sat upon him was called Faithful and True, and **in righteousness** he does judge and **make war**" (Revelation 19:11).

Yes, Jesus judges and make war in righteousness. That is, when a person partakes of the righteousness of Jesus and lives righteously, a righteous life automatically makes war; and thus, persecution from the enemies of Jesus' Church may arise. However, there is more to the warrior priesthood. Through spiritual weapons the priesthood fights spiritual forces, and sometimes using those same spiritual weapons, the priesthood defeats its natural enemies. That is, the Melchizedek priesthood can make war that results in physical slaughters without using physical hands. We are entering an era in which Jesus' saints worldwide will have to defend the gospel through spiritual weapons.

Mouth-Sword

Revelation 19:15-16; 21, BSB: [15] *And* **from His mouth proceeds a sharp sword** *with which to strike down the nations, and He will rule them with an iron scepter. He treads the winepress of the fury of the wrath of God, the Almighty.* [16] *And He has a name* *written on His robe and on His thigh .... ²¹And the rest were killed with the **sword that proceeded from the mouth** of the One seated on the horse.*

*2 Thessalonians 2:8: And then shall that 'Lawless' be revealed, whom the Lord shall consume with the **spirit of his mouth** ....*

Jesus, the King of Kings made war in righteousness against His enemies; and he killed some of them with the sword of his mouth. In other words, the Melchizedek priesthood will experience enemies, however, our weapon to counter any attacks will not be through using physical weapons, yet our weapons can cause physical death.

*Daniel 8:25: And through his policy also he shall cause craft to prosper in his hand; and he shall magnify himself in his heart, and by peace shall destroy many: he shall also stand up against the Prince of princes; **but he shall be broken without hand.***

Daniel 8 prefigures the beast (a king) to come. In that chapter, Daniel indicated that this king would eventually stand up against the "Prince of princes." This "Prince of princes" is Jesus who is also called the "King of kings and the Lord of Lords." And as in Revelation 19, the kings who **confederate or unionized** with the beast-king was destroyed with the sword of Jesus mouth, this beast-king shall be "broken without hand."

In other words, Jesus does not use physical weapon to destroy His enemies. He uses spiritual weapons, weapons that can destroy **"without hand."** Jesus used the sword of His mouth, or the "Spirit of His mouth" to destroy His enemies. Paul used a similar weapon, "words" to release the hand of the Lord!

The Hand of the Lord

Acts 13:4-12: ⁴So they, being sent forth by the Holy 'Spirit,' departed unto Seleucia; and from there they sailed to Cyprus. ⁵And when they were at Salamis, they preached the word of God *in the synagogues of the Jews: and they had also John to their minister. ⁶And when they had gone through the isle unto Paphos, they found a certain sorcerer, a false prophet, a Jew, whose name was Barjesus: ⁷Which was with the deputy of the country, Sergius Paulus, a prudent man; who called for Barnabas and Saul, and desired to hear the word of God. ⁸But Elymas the sorcerer (for so is his name by interpretation) withstood them, seeking to turn away the deputy from the faith. ⁹Then Saul, (who also is called Paul,) filled with the Holy 'Spirit,' set his eyes on him, ¹⁰**And said,** O full of all subtilty and all mischief, you 'son' of the devil, you enemy of all righteousness, wilt you not cease to pervert the right ways of the Lord? ¹¹And now, behold, **the hand of the Lord is upon you,** and you shall be blind, not seeing the sun for a season. And immediately there fell on him a mist and a darkness; and he went about seeking some to lead him by the hand. ¹²Then the deputy, when he saw what was done, believed, being astonished at the doctrine of the Lord.*

Paul encountered a sorcerer who was a son (mature son) of the Devil, and an enemy of all righteousness (not just some righteousness, but **all** righteousness). Paul's response was not to use a physical weapon to stop this sorcerer. On the contrary, he used words to declare that God's hands would judge the sorcerer, not physical hands. "Then Saul, (who also is called Paul,) filled with the Holy 'Spirit,' set his eyes on him, ¹⁰And **said** ... behold, **the hand of the Lord** is upon you, and **you shall be blind,** not seeing the sun for a season. **And immediately there fell on him a mist and a darkness;** and he went about seeking some to lead him by the hand."

The "hand of the Lord" is not a physical hand. So, Paul did not get physical with the magi. According to Jesus, the finger of God is the Spirit of God! According to the prophet Ezekiel, God's hand is the Spirit.

*Matthew 12:28: But if I cast out devils by **the Spirit of God,** then the kingdom of God is come unto you.*

*Luke 11:20: But if I with the **finger of God** cast out devils, no doubt the kingdom of God is come upon you*

*Ezekiel 8:3: And he **put forth the form of a hand** and took me by a lock of mine head; and **the Spirit lifted** me up between the earth and the heaven and brought me in the visions of God to Jerusalem.*

Matthew indicated that Jesus cast our demons with the Spirit of God. Luke's account equated the Spirit of God with the "finger of God." Ezekiel also wrote that the Spirit is like the form of a hand. Thus, God can manifest His Holy Spirit as a hand. The Melchizedek ministry is a ministry that does not uses physical weapons to make war. Jesus spoke and it affected people. He spoke words and people were healed. He spoke words and His enemies would fall before Him.

*2 Corinthians 10:3-4: [3]For though we walk in the flesh, we do not war 'according to' the flesh: [4](For **the weapons** of our warfare are not 'fleshly', but mighty through God to the pulling down of strong holds).*

*John 18:4-6: [4]Jesus therefore, knowing all things that should come upon him, went forth, and **said** unto them, who seek you? [5]They answered him, Jesus of Nazareth. Jesus says to them, **I am.** And Judas also, which betrayed him, stood with them. [6]As soon then as he had **said** to them, I am, **they went backward, and fell to the ground.***

The Day of His Wrath

*Psalms 110:4-5: [4]The LORD has sworn, and will not repent, you are **a priest forever after the order of Melchizedek.** [5]The Lord at your right hand shall strike through kings in **the day of his wrath.***

Revelation 6:15-17: [15]And the kings of the earth, and the great men, and the rich men, and the chief captains, and the mighty men, and every bondman, and every free man, hid themselves in *the dens and in the rocks of the mountains; ¹⁶And said to the mountains and rocks, fall on us, and hide us from the face of him that sits on the throne, and from the wrath of the Lamb: ¹⁷For the great **day of his wrath** is come; and who shall be able to stand?*

*Job 20:28-29: ²⁸The increase of his house shall depart, and his goods shall flow away in **the day of his wrath**. ²⁹This is the portion of a wicked man from God, and the heritage appointed unto him by God.*

The phrase "day of his wrath" is used three (3) times in the Bible. In Job, the phrase is used in conjunction with the wicked losing the increase of his house. In the book of Revelation, the day of his wrath is connected to the Sixth Seal and the wrath of the Lamb of God. In Psalms 110 it is used in relation to Melchizedek in the day the Lord will strike through kings.

That is, the Melchizedek ministry also involves things that are not necessarily pleasant. The Melchizedek ministry must also execute God's judgment in the earth; and this is not a happy thing to do. All through the book of Revelation, we see the priest's office being executed by prophet-priests meeting out God's judgments. So, without going into detail, I will cite some examples to show that the work in the book of Revelation relates to priesthood of the Melchizedek order.

In Revelation 1:6, John in his introduction, in the book of Revelation, stated that God "has made us kings and priests unto God and His Father."[4] Thus, the book of Revelation is to also be taught from the "king-priest ministry" relating to the order of Melchizedek. In Revelation 5:10, the believers are called "kings and priests" (or "a kingdom of priests"), again reinforcing the "kingly priesthood" ministry in the book of Revelation.

---

[4] The Alexandrian texts (some of the oldest texts) reads: "and he has made us a kingdom, priests to God and his Father ...."

Throughout the book of Revelation, we read about the twenty-four (24) elders around God's throne. Twenty-four (24) is the number that correspond to priesthood. In 1 Chronicles 24, David divided the ministry of the priests into twenty-four courses.

In Revelation 8, the angel ministering at the Altar of Incense is a picture of Jesus, our High Priest, ministering "to" and ministering "with" the prayer of all the saints; and protecting the saints through the prayers of all the saints. In Revelation 8 through Revelation 11, the angels with the seven trumpets sounding judgments in the earth also represents the prophet-priest ministry. That is, in Joshua 6:4, it was seven priests with seven trumpets who led the people of God to execute judgment on the wall of Jericho; and eventually defeating the "unbeliever" of Jericho; yet saving the "believer" Rahab, the prostitute.

In Revelation 11, the two candlesticks and the two olive trees directly relate to the candlestick in the tabernacle Moses built; and the two cherubs made of two olive trees in the temple Solomon built; and is therefore related to the priesthood. In Revelation 15 though Revelation 16, the seven angels with the seven bowls of the seven last plagues filled with God's wrath came out of the temple of God with these plagues. Only priests can go in and out of the temple. Revelation 22:7-9 teaches that the angels with the bowls filled with God' wrath are also prophet-priests ministering God's judgments. Revelation 20:4-6, specifically states that the ministry of the resurrected saints, will be as priests and kings.

With that said, the Church need to change her view of her ministry in the earth to now function in Jesus' Melchizedek ministry, as kings and priest. That is, there is a current call to preach Jesus and Him crucified; there is a current call to execute God judgments in the earth through the priest's office, as God's wills it; there is a call to be priests in the day of His wrath.

Priest Reveals the Yes!

*Psalms 110:4: The LORD has sworn, and will not repent, You are a **priest** forever after the **order of Melchizedek.***

The Hebrew word for priest is "kohen" [(כהן). reading from left to right]. Priest is associated with the Hebrew word for "yes." The Hebrew word for yes is KeN (כן), which means "yes," or "it is so." "KeN" ("it is so") was first used relative to the Creator's words producing what was declared to be.

*Genesis 1:9: And God said, let the waters under the heaven be gathered together unto one place, and let the dry land appear: and **it was so.***

Thus, the Hebrew word "KoHen" is "KeN" with an "H" inserted in the middle. The pictographic idea of the Hebrew letter "H" (ה) is the picture of an **open window, or an opening, and "hey" (revealed to attract attention).** When this Hebrew letter "H" is used at the end of a Hebrew word, it makes that word feminine. However, when this letter "H" (ה) is used in the middle of a word, it means **to reveal,** to reveal the heart, to behold, and to look.

It follows that KoHeN means to reveal the "yes." That is, the priest reveals what God says "yes" to. The priest reveals God's creative words that accomplishes ("it is so") what He has said. Therefore, the Melchizedek priesthood is to function in a place of knowing and relaying what God says "yes" to, whether his "yes" means bad or good outcome. We must remain faithful to His "KoHen."

*2 Corinthians 1:18-20, BSB: [18]But as surely as God is faithful, our message to you is not "Yes" and "No." [19]For the Son of God, Jesus Christ, who was proclaimed among you by me and Silvanusc and Timothy, was not "Yes" and "No," but **in Him it has always** been **"Yes."** [20]For all the promises of God are **"Yes"** in*

Christ. And so, through Him, our "Amen" is spoken to the glory of God.

*Malachi: 2:7, BSB: For the lips of a **priest** should preserve knowledge, and **people should seek instruction from his mouth**, because he is the messenger of the LORD of Hosts."*

In conclusion, the Melchizedek ministry is a ministry that has the answers. The foremost answer is that Jesus and Him crucified is the Answer of humanity's problems, from beginning to end. The royal priesthood is to strive to have relevant and specific prophetic answers from our Lord Jesus Christ for those in need of answers! Answers that reveals to those seeking what God says "yes" to! Answers that causes faith in God's "KoHen"—Jesus, the Son of God, the Great Hight Priests according to the order of Melchizedek!

Other Books

Poiema, by Judith Peart

Wisdom from Above, by Judith Peart

Procreation, Understanding Sex, and Identity, by Judith Peart

100 Nevers, by Judith Peart

The Shattered and the Healing by Judith Peart

The Lamb, by Donald Peart

Jesus' Resurrection, Our Inheritance, by Donald Peart.

Sexuality, By Donald Peart

Forgiven 490 Times, by Donald Peart w/Judith Peart!

The Days of the Seventh Angel, By Donald Peart

The Torah (The Principle) of Giving, by Donald Peart

The Time Came, by Donald Peart

The Last Hour, the First Hour, the Forty-Second Generation, by Donald Peart

Vision Real, by Donald Peart

The False Prophet, Alias, Another Beast V1, by Donald Peart

"the beast," by Donald Peart

Son of Man Prophesy Against the false prophet, by Donald Peart

The Dragon's Tail, the Prophets who Teaches Lies, by Donald Peart

The Work of Lawlessness Revealed, by Donald Peart

When the Lord Made the Tempter, by Donald Peart

Examining Doctrine, Volume 1, by Donald Peart

Exousia, Your God Given Authority, by Donald Peart

The Numbers of God, by Donald Peart

The Completions of the Ages ... by Donald Peart

The Revelation of Jesus Christ, by Donald Peart

Jude—Translation and Commentary, by Donald Peart

Obtaining the Better Resurrection, by Donald Peart

Manifestations from Our Lord Jesus ...by Donald and Judith Peart).

Obtaining the Better Resurrection, by Donald Peart

The New Testament, Dr. Donald Peart Exegesis

The Tree of Life, By Dr. Donald Peart

The Spirit and Power of John, the Baptist by Dr. Donald Peart

The Shattered and the Healing by Judith Peart

Is She Married to a Husband? by Donald Peart

The Ugliest Man God Made by Donald Peart

Does Answering the Call of God Impact Your Children? by Donald Peart
Victory Out-of-the Beast-the Harvest of the Earth by Donald Peart
The Order of Melchizedek by Donald Peart
Ezekiel-the House-the City-the Land (Interpreting the Patterns), by Donald Peart
Butter and Honey (Understanding How to Choose the Good and Refuse Evil), by Donald Peart
Wholly Maturing and Wholly Inheriting, Spirit, Soul, and Body, by Donald Peart
Angels and the Supernatural, by Donald Peart

Contact Information:

Crown of Glory Ministries
P.O. Box 1041 Randallstown, MD 21133
donaldpeart7@gmail.com

Made in the USA
Middletown, DE
26 August 2024

59733898R00054